Sharing Circles:

Guided Discussions for Developing Character

Susanna Palomares & David Cowan

INNERCHOICE Publishing

Cover Design – Linda Thille

Copyright © 2001, Innerchoice Publishing • All rights reserved
(Revised Edition, 2010)

ISBN – 10: 1-56499-062-4
ISBN – 13: 978-1-56499-062-4

INNERCHOICE Publishing
15079 Oak Chase Court
Wellington, FL 33414

www.InnerchoicePublishing.com

Any reproduction by any means and for any purpose whatsoever is explicitly prohibited without written permission. Requests for such permission should be directed to INNERCHOICE PUBLISHING.

"Intelligence, plus character, that is the goal of true education."

Dr. Martin Luther King, Jr.

Contents

EDUCATING FOR CHARACTER 1
SHARING CIRCLES: THE CHARACTER EDUCATION SUPER STRATEGY 7
WHAT YOU NEED TO KNOW ABOUT SHARING CIRCLES 11
HOW TO LEAD A SHARING CIRCLE 15

Sharing Circle Topics

I Told the Truth and Was Glad 23
A Hero Or Heroine I Admire 24
I Respected Myself for Something I Did 25
A Time I Showed Someone That I Cared 26
What It Means to Live By the Golden Rule 27
How I Show That I'm a Good School Citizen 28
A Rule We Have In My Family 29
A Character Trait I Admire in Others 30
Someone I Know Who Is an Accepting Person 31
Someone Who Trusts Me 32
When Someone Criticized Me 33
A Time I Kept My Promise 34
One of the Nicest Things a Friend Ever Did for Me 35
Someone Helped Me When I Needed and Wanted Help 36
Something I'm Learning Now That Is Difficult 37
A Way I Earned Something and What I Did With It 38
A Responsible Habit I've Developed 39
A Time I Was Afraid, But I Did It Anyway 40
I Stood Up for Something I Strongly Believe In 41
How I Helped Someone Who Was Having a Problem 42
It Was Hard to Say No, But I Did 43
What I Think Good Communication Is 44
What I Value Most in a Friend 45
What I Do When the Going Gets Tough 45
An Ability or Talent I'm Proud Of 47
Something I Enjoy Doing Because It Gives Me a Feeling of Accomplishment 48
I Thought Over My Decision, and I Stuck to It 49
When One Person Kept Blaming Another for Causing a Problem 50
I Got Blamed for Something I Didn't Do 51
A Time Someone Put Me Down, But I Handled It Well 52
How I Made Someone Feel Happy 53
Someone I Learned To Trust 54
Something I Finished That I Had a Hard Time Starting 55
A Time I Was Involved in a Misunderstanding 56
Something That Really Bothers Me 57
I Got Involved in a Conflict Because Something Unfair Was Happening to Someone Else 58
A Time I Controlled Myself and the Situation Well 59
How I Handled a Disagreement with a Friend 60
We Made Room For One More 61
I Wanted To Be Part of a Group, But Was Left Out 62

A Situation in Which I Behaved Responsibly	63
A Time I Talked to Someone I Was Afraid to Talk To	64
Someone Handled a Problem Differently Than I'd Have Handled It	65
An Experience That Caused Me to See Things Differently	66
How I Learned to Get Along With Someone Who Doesn't Think the Way I Do	67
Two Things I Believe In That Conflict With Each Other	68
A Time When I Trusted Myself	69
I Made a Decision Based on My Values	70
An Agreement That Was Hard to Keep	71
I Didn't Do Something Because I Knew It Would Hurt Someone	72
Something Nice I Did for a Friend	73
Someone Did Something for Me That I Appreciated	74
Something I Taught Myself	75
What Good Friends Need From Each Other	76
I Had a Hard Time Choosing Between Two Things	77
How I Showed Someone That I Could Be Trusted	78
A Time When I Misunderstood What Someone Said	79
How I Would Like To Be Known by Others	80
I Reached Out To Someone Who Needed A Friend	81
A Time I Was Really Angry, But I Was Able To Calm Myself Down	82
Someone Who Demonstrated a Lot of Courage	83
A Good Choice That I'm Glad I Made	84
I Did Something That Made Me Feel Like a Good Person	85
A Time Someone Was Being Treated Unfairly	86
A Time When I Accepted Someone Else's Feelings	87
How I Deal with Intolerance and Prejudice	88
What I Think the World Needs To Be a Better Place	89
Something I've Done (or Could Do) to Improve Our World	90
One of My Favorite Possessions	91
How I Feel About War	92
It Made Me Feel Good to Make Someone Else Feel Good	93
I Had a Problem and Solved It	94
Things I Do To Keep a Friend	95
People Seem to Respect Me When...	96
Somebody Whose Opinion I Value Very Much	97
An Important Person in My Life	98
I Succeeded Because I Encouraged Myself	99
Someone Tried to Make Me Do Something I Didn't Want to Do	100
A Significant Event in My Life	101
Something I Want to Keep	102
My Greatest Asset	103
Part of Me Wanted to Do One Thing, and Part of Me Wanted to Do Another	104
I Said Yes When I Wanted to Say No	105
A Way in Which I'm Responsible	106
A Time I Disappointed Someone	107
A Time I Used Good Judgement	108
It Was Difficult, But I Controlled Myself	109
Someone in Authority Whom I Respect	110
I Could Have Hurt Someone's Feelings, But I Didn't	111
A Time I Accepted and Included Someone	112
A Promise That Was Hard to Keep	113
I Said No Because It Was the Right Thing to Do	114
How My Mistake Helped Me Learn	115

Educating for Character

Why Educate for Character?

Because we don't just want smart kids, we want good kids. Education has always attempted to develop good people. Even during periods when educators were told that they *must not* teach values, they did anyway. They modeled kindness, caring, and respect; punished cheating, stealing, and lying; rewarded industriousness; and emphasized the importance of good citizenship in the context of a just and fair school community.

Responsible behavior begins with ethical thinking, and helping students to think — to solve problems, make decisions and render judgments — is clearly the job of the school. Along with language, math, science, and art, schools must teach acceptable standards of conduct, and the attitudes and attributes that foster them. Smart is not enough to sustain the principles and belief systems upon which our society is built. Good also belongs in this picture.

Because to some degree good comes before smart. To consistently do their best work, students must value excellence, even if it's just an excellent grade. Few students can do well in school without work, and work requires diligence. If every child came to school with well developed senses of responsibility, honesty, integrity, and fairness, teaching would be easy. But since, both practically and developmentally, this is impossible, schools are left with no choice but to instill values right along with the other basics. They always have. They always will. The difference is that today many schools are again teaching values deliberately — through the curriculum.

According to Lawrence Kohlberg and others who have done extensive research on moral development, elementary-age children are primarily concerned with their own survival — avoiding punishment and obtaining rewards by obeying the rules. Older children are motivated by the desire to gain approval from others (principally peers) and avoid disapproval. Only at the highest level of moral development are rules interpreted in terms of self-chosen principles.

The strong influence of the home in preschool years gives way to the broader world of the school and peer group as children enter school. Educators are not usurping a family mandate by teaching moral values; the children carry the mandate with them, right out the door and into the school. They are whole people, and schools cannot deal with their minds apart from their morality.

Because somebody's got to do it. Knowing that so many children lack role models and caring adults in their lives, and knowing, as a consequence, that society is in real danger, the educational system would be negligent were it not to respond. To some, character education will seem like just one more job added to the educator's overwhelming list of responsibilities. But it's a critically important job — and somebody's got to do it.

What Is Good Character?

In, *Educating for Character* (Bantam, 1991), psychologist and educator Thomas Lickona states that good character consists of "knowing the good, desiring the good, and doing the good — habits of mind, habits of heart, and habits of action." In other words, a morally mature person knows what is right, cares deeply about what is right, and does what is right.

What Values Should We Teach?

Many educators today recall being told never to venture into the values arena under any circumstances. To those educators, the current interest in character education must seem rather ironic. Does our concern for morality skip whole decades? What happened?

The short answer is this: While trying to meet the educational needs of an increasingly pluralistic society, educators went through a period of several years wherein no one was sure whose values to teach. With so many cultures, languages, and ethnic groups to accommodate, schools thought it best to leave the entire issue of values alone. Developing character was the job of families, supported by their religious institutions. Unfortunately, both families and religious institutions were losing their sway over young people during that same period of time.

Today, educators are not so worried about "whose values to teach," and are acknowledging that every person needs to acquire certain character attributes and be guided by universal moral values—values that unite all people everywhere because they affirm basic human worth and dignity.

Universal moral values underlie the 1948 United Nations Universal Declaration of Human Rights, which calls for:

- life
- liberty
- freedom from personal attack
- freedom from slavery
- recognition before the law and the presumption of innocence until proven guilty
- freedom from torture
- freedom of conscience and religion
- freedom of expression
- privacy, family, and correspondence
- freedom to participate freely in community life
- education
- a standard of living adequate for maintaining health and well being

What Schools Can Do

Everything about a school reflects to some degree that school's current set of values. The way administrators lead and teachers manage their classes, the way grades are awarded and sports programs are administered, the way hallways and playgrounds are monitored all send moral messages. These messages, picked up by students on super sensitive receivers, significantly affect character development.

Much of what students learn is learned by imitation or modeling. The younger the student, the stronger the impact of models on development. For this reason, the values that you choose to teach, model, and talk about should extend to all aspects of school life.

The experiences generated by being a member of the school community are much more character-forming than anything an individual educator can say on the subject of morality or ethics. Ask regularly: *What lessons are being taught by the way our school operates on a daily basis?*

Does your school...

1. have a philosophy statement clearly outlining character expectations for all members of the school community? Is it posted prominently and a visible part of school life? If you are a teacher or counselor, do you have a compatible philosophy statement for your classroom or counseling center?
2. provide all students with clear academic and behavior goals?
3. have a discipline policy that supports the character goals of the school?
4. encourage students to participate in formal school and/or community service projects?
5. have available to students on a regular basis general school service activities, e.g., teacher aides,

messengers, tutors, guest greeters, fund-raising, school clean up, etc.?

6. have a range of extracurricular activities led by school staff and supported by parents and community, e.g., sports, band, choir, drama, art club?

Do you...

1. demonstrate character traits and pro-social habits that are supportive of the school philosophy and goals? Do other faculty, administrators, and certified staff also effectively model these goals and philosophy?
2. see a relationship between the way you treat students and the way they treat each other?
3. have an awareness of how small actions model and teach?
4. share concern for the well-being of others — both students and staff?
5. give extra help to students who need it?
6. counsel and/or teach enthusiastically?
7. come to your classes or counseling group prepared to lead activities?
8. return students work in a timely manner?
9. refrain from gossiping or criticizing students, parents, or administrators?

What Counselors and Teachers Can Do

Moral values are already so tightly woven into the fabric of school life that we no longer see the individual threads. The environment of the school is rich with values. The question is: which values?

It is who we are as well as what we say that builds character in children. Students learn from what they observe and experience in the environment; they develop the values that you model.

All students, and particularly at-risk students, need consistent caring in the form of support and encouragement. They must know that you believe they can overcome obstacles and that you are depending on them to make ethical, pro-social choices.

The Model:

- Treat students with love and respect; set a good example.
- Share your moral convictions with students.
- Talk about community service you perform.
- Establish clear academic and moral goals for your class.
- Present well-planned lessons or counseling sessions.

- Counsel or teach enthusiastically.
- Return homework and test papers promptly.
- Don't gossip about students or colleagues.
- Show consideration for other educators.
- Go the extra mile for a student who is struggling.
- Be observant of teachable moments.

The Words

- State character goals as positive imperatives, e.g., "Be on time," "Treat others fairly," "Do your best work," "Keep your word." Avoid negative wording, such as "Don't be late," "Don't be unkind," and "Never break a promise."
- Teach values directly. Use the words (i.e., *trustworthiness*, *respect*, *responsibility*, *caring*, etc.), write and define them, identify the behaviors in which they are embodied, and have students practice those behaviors.

The Environment

- Help students know each other, respect and care about each other, and experience a sense of full inclusion in the group.
- Through cooperative learning, teach children to help each other and work together.
- Display pictures, portraits of worthy individuals, posters, and quotations that reflect the high moral purpose and goals of your school.
- Teach values in conjunction with parents and community.

The Management

- Use the creation and enforcement of rules as opportunities to foster moral reasoning.
- Instill civic values by holding class meetings to discuss problems that arise.
- Involve students in decision making and shared responsibility for making the classroom a positive place to learn.

The Skills

- Teach a decision-making process that encourages students to make conscious choices from among alternatives that have been examined not only for their relative effectiveness in achieving a stated goal, but for their moral consequences.
- Teach skills of listening, communication, assertiveness, problem solving, conflict resolution, and refusal/resistance.
- Give students many opportunities to make choices.

The Academics

- Use academic subjects as a vehicle for examining ethical issues.

- Foster academic responsibility and regard for the value of learning and work.
- Encourage moral reflection through reading, writing, discussion.
- Give students opportunities to respond to moral issues.

How This Book Can Help

Sharing Circles provide opportunities for students to engage in dialog regarding ethics, values and character. The Sharing Circle process is an extremely powerful process for ethical and moral reflection. Part of its value for this purpose lies in the fact that it is guided by an established procedure and a specific topic. In addition, the process requires that students demonstrate such things as respect, responsibility, trust, caring and fairness as a condition of participating.

Because character is demonstrated in the simple elements of everyday life, when you and your students discuss something like "A Good Choice That I'm Glad I Made," or "Something Nice I Did For A Friend," you are touching on character in all its dimensions and nuances. You are able to view, reflect on and learn character through connecting it to everyday thoughts, feelings, and behaviors. Therefore, this book provides a wide variety of topics. Some dealing directly with a recognized character trait and others getting at character through an indirect approach. The character connections come about through the responses of the students both in the sharing phase and as they refect on and answer the discussion questions and engage in discussion. The following pages provide additional information regarding the power of the Sharing Circle process for developing character.

Sharing Circles:
The Character Education Super Strategy

Sharing Circles are a unique small-group process in which participants (including the leader) share their feelings, experiences, and insights in response to specific, assigned topics. Sharing Circles are loosely structured, and participants are expected to adhere to rules that promote the goals of positive interaction while specifically assuring cooperation, effective communication, trust, and confidentiality.

Character develops within a social environment. The social nature of the Sharing Circle environment — the messages it sends to students and the behaviors it encourages and discourages — are highly conducive to character development. Students follow clear rules of conduct, accept ownership of those rules, are supportive of one another, and experience satisfaction by complying with established guidelines and procedures. Regular use of Sharing Circles can noticeably accelerate the development and internalization of the moral values addressed in this book.

Two Initial Pointers

To prepare yourself to take full advantage of the Sharing Circle process, thoroughly read and digest the section entitled How to Lead a Sharing Circle which begins on page 15. As you are reading, keep two points in mind:

First, the topic elaborations provided under the heading, "Introducing the Topic," are guides for you to follow when presenting the topic to your students. They are excellent models, but need not be read verbatim. The idea is to focus the attention of students on the specific topic to be discussed. *In your elaboration, try to use language and examples that are appropriate to the age, ability and culture of your students.*

Second, we strongly urge you to respect the integrity of the sharing and discussion phases of the Sharing Circle process. These two phases are procedurally and qualitatively different, yet of equal importance in promoting awareness, insight and higher-level thinking in students.

After you have led several Sharing Circles, you will appreciate the instructional advantage of maintaining this unique relationship between the sharing and discussion phases.

In the sharing phase each circle member (adult leader, too) has the opportunity to take one turn to respond to the topic. In the discussion phase questions are asked and all circle members engage in a free-flowing exchange of thoughts and ideas.

During the sharing phase, the topic is intended to prompt awareness and insight through voluntary sharing and the self-reflective thought process of talking about oneself. This growing self-understanding is encouraged by sharing in a socially-safe environment where others are attentively listening.

In the discussion phase students are guided to understand what has been shared at deeper levels, to evaluate ideas that have been generated by the topic in the sharing phase, and to apply specific concepts to other areas of learning.

With the teacher or counselor (or other adult leader) serving as a guide to discovery students are engaged in self-reflective learning and critical inquiry.

All guided discussion topics are intended to develop awareness and insight through voluntary sharing. This occurs in the first (or sharing) phase of the process. The discussion phase, for which specific questions are provided, allows students to understand what has been shared at deeper levels, to evaluate ideas that have been generated by the topic, and to apply specific concepts to other areas of learning.

How Sharing Circles Help Students Develop Moral Awareness

As students follow the rules and relate to each other verbally during Sharing Circles, they are practicing respectful listening and oral communication. Through insights gained in the course of pondering and discussing the various topics, students become more aware of what constitutes good character as well as the need to develop control of their feelings, thoughts, and behaviors. Through the positive experience of give and take, they also learn the importance of interacting responsibly and effectively.

The Sharing Circle topics offered in this book address both moral values and important skills — keeping agreements, developing responsible habits, solving problems, demonstrating respect for self and others, being loyal, being trustworthy and honest, following rules, demonstrating kindness and consideration, resolving conflicts, etc.

Topics like these not only help students identify specific values, they provide a venue within which students can use the "language of character," and they require students to describe incidents and behaviors from their own experience that illustrate those values.

This book includes a wide variety of topics. While some deal with specific character traits (e.g., "How I Show Respect"), most deal with subjects that *indirectly* impact character. Character, after all, is developed within the context of all life experiences. When good character traits are internalized, children behave in ethical ways without having to constantly think about being respectful, trustworthy or fair. In most situations they are able to choose good behavior without conscious deliberation. They simply live it.

Sharing Circles allow students to confront difficult decision-making situations. In response to the topics posed, students are asked to state positions, to think about their reasons for selecting those positions, and to listen to the positions and reasoning of others.

Sharing Circles are a perfect vehicle for educating both the mind and the heart.

Learning Right from Wrong

As students learn to relate effectively to others, moral issues surface again and again. Students learn that all people have the power to influence one another. They become aware not only of how others affect them, but of the effects their behaviors have on others.

The Sharing Circle process has been designed so that healthy, responsible behaviors are modeled by the teacher or counselor in his or her role as leader. Also, the rules require that the students relate responsibly and effectively to one another. Sharing Circles bring out and affirm the positive qualities inherent in everyone and allow students to practice effective modes of communication. Because Sharing Circles provide a place where participants are listened to and their feelings accepted, students learn how to provide the same conditions to peers and adults outside the Sharing Circle.

Sharing Circles teach cooperation. As equitably as possible, the discussion structure attempts to meet the needs of all participants. Everyone's feelings are accepted; everyone's contributions are judged valuable. The Sharing Circle group is not another competitive arena, but is guided by a spirit of collaboration.

When students practice fair, respectful interaction with one another, they benefit from the experience and are likely to employ these responsible behaviors in other life situations.

Practicing Responsible Behaviors

A great benefit of Sharing Circles is that they do not merely teach young people about social interaction, they let them interact! Every Sharing Circle is a real-life experience of social interaction where the students share, listen, explore, plan and problem solve together. As they interact, they learn about each other and they realize what it takes to relate respectfully and honestly with others. Any given Sharing Circle may provide a dozen tiny flashes of positive interpersonal insight for an individual participant. Gradually, the reality of what constitutes responsible behavior in relating to others is internalized.

Through this sharing of interpersonal experiences, students learn that behavior can be positive or negative, and sometimes both at the same time. Consequences can be constructive, destructive, or both. Different people respond differently to the same event. They have different feelings and thoughts. The students begin to understand what will cause what to happen; they grasp the concept of cause and effect; they see themselves affecting others and being affected by others.

The ability to make accurate interpretations and responses in social situations allows students to know where they stand with themselves and with others. They can tell what actions "fit" a situation. Sharing Circles are marvelous testing grounds where students can observe themselves and others in action, and can begin to see themselves as contributing to the good and bad feelings of others. With this understanding, students are helped to conclude that being responsible towards others feels good, and is the most valuable and personally rewarding form of interaction.

What You Need to Know About Sharing Circles

Group Size and Composition

This is a time for focusing on individuals' contributions in an unhurried fashion. For this reason, each Sharing Circle session needs to be kept relatively small—eight to twelve usually works best. Once they move beyond the primary grades, students are capable of extensive verbalization. You will want to encourage this, and not stifle them because of time constraints.

Each group should be as heterogeneous as possible with respect to sex, ability, and racial/ethnic background. Sometimes there will be a group in which all the students are particularly reticent to speak. At these times, bring in an expressive student or two who will get things going. Sometimes it is necessary for practical reasons to change the membership of a group. Once established, however, it is advisable to keep a group as stable as possible.

Length and Location

Most sessions last approximately 10 to 20 minutes. At first students tend to be reluctant to express themselves fully because they do not yet know that this is a safe place. Consequently your first sessions may not last more than 10 minutes. Generally speaking, students become comfortable and motivated to speak with continued experience.

In middle- and high-school classrooms, Sharing Circles may be conducted at any time during the class period. Starting circle sessions at the beginning of the period allows additional time in case students become deeply involved in the topic. If you start late in the period, make sure the students are aware of their responsibility to be concise.

In elementary classes, any time of day is appropriate for Sharing Circles. Some teachers like to set the tone for the day by beginning with this process; others feel it's a perfect way to complete the day and to send the students away with positive feelings.

Sharing Circles may be carried out wherever there is room for students to sit in a circle and experience few or no distractions. Most leaders prefer to have students sit in chairs rather than on the floor. Students seem to be less apt to invade one another's space while seated in chairs. Some leaders conduct sessions outdoors, with students seated in a secluded, grassy area.

How to Involve All the Students

Teachers and counselors have used numerous methods to involve students in Sharing Circles. What works well for one leader or class does not always work for another. Here are two basic strategies leaders have successfully used to get groups started. Whichever you use, we recommend that you post a chart listing the rules and procedures to which every participant may refer.

1. Divide the class into groups of 8 to 12 students. Start one group at a time and cycle through all groups. If possible, provide an opportunity for every student to experience a Sharing Circle in a setting where there are no disturbances. This may mean arranging for another staff member or aide to take charge of the students not participating in the Sharing Circle. Non-participants may work on course work or silent reading, or if you have a cooperative librarian, they may be sent to the library to work independently or in small groups on a class assignment. Repeat this procedure until all of the students have been involved in at least one circle session.

Next, initiate a class discussion about the process. Explain that from now on you will be meeting with each Sharing Circle group in the classroom, with the remainder of the class present. Ask the students to help you plan established procedures for the remainder of the class to follow.

Meet with each Sharing Circle group on a different day, systematically cycling through the groups.

2. Combine an inner discussion group with an outer circle. Conduct a Sharing Circle with the inner group while those in the outer group listen and observe. Then have the two groups change places, with the students on the outside becoming the inner discussion group, and responding verbally to the topic. If you run out of time in middle- or high-school classrooms, use two class periods for this. Later, a third group may be added to this alternating cycle. The end product of this arrangement is two or more groups (comprising everyone in the class) meeting together simultaneously. While one group is involved in discussion, the other groups listen and observe as members of an outer group.

What To Do With the Rest of the Class

A number of arrangements can be made for students who are not participating in Sharing Circles. Here are some ideas:

- Arrange the room to ensure privacy. This may involve placing a circle of chairs or carpeting in a corner, away from other work areas. You might construct dividers from existing furniture, such as bookshelves or screens, or simply arrange chairs and tables in such a way that the Sharing Circle discussion area is protected from distractions.

- Involve aides, counselors, parents, or fellow teachers. Have an aide conduct a lesson with the rest of the class while you meet with a Sharing Circle group. If you do not have an aide assigned to you, use auxiliary staff or parent volunteers.

- Have students work quietly on subject-area assignments in pairs or small, task-oriented groups.

- Utilize student aides or leaders. If the seat-work activity is in a content area, appoint students who show ability in that area as "consultants," and have them assist other students.

- Give the students plenty to do. List academic activities on the board. Make materials for quiet individual activities available so that students cannot run out of things to do and be tempted to consult you or disturb others.

- Make the activity of students outside the Sharing Circle group enjoyable. When you can involve the rest of the class in something meaningful to them, students will probably be less likely to interrupt the discussion.

- Have the students work on an ongoing project. When they have a task in progress, students can simply resume where they left off, with little or no introduction from you. In these cases, appointing a "person in charge," "group leader," or "consultant" is wise.

- Allow individual journal-writing. While a Sharing Circle is in progress, have the other students make entries in a private (or share-with-teacher-only) journal. The topic for journal writing could be the same topic that is being discussed in the Sharing Circle. Do not correct the journals, but if you read them, be sure to respond to the entries with your own written thoughts, where appropriate.

How to Lead a Sharing Circle

This section is a thorough guide for conducting Sharing Circles. It covers major points to keep in mind and answers questions which will arise as you begin using the program. Please remember that these guidelines are presented to assist you, not to restrict you. Follow them, and trust your own leadership style at the same time.

The Sharing Circle is a structured communication process that provides students a safe place for learning about life and developing important aspects of social-emotional learning.

First, we'll provide a brief overview of the process of leading a Sharing Circle and then we'll cover each step in more detail.

A Sharing Circle begins when a group of students and the adult leader sit down together in a circle so that each person is able to see the others easily. The leader of the Sharing Circle briefly greets and welcomes each individual, conveying a feeling of enthusiasm blended with seriousness.

When everyone appears comfortable, the leader takes a few moments to review the Sharing Circle Rules. These rules inform the students of the positive behaviors required of them and guarantees the emotional safety and security, and equality of each member.

After the students understand and agree to follow the rules, the leader announces the topic for the session. A brief elaboration of the topic follows in which the leader provides examples and possibly mentions the topics relationship to prior topics or to other things the students are involved in. Then the leader re-states the topic and allows a little silence during which circle members may review and ponder their own related memories and mentally prepare their verbal response to the topic. (The topics and elaborations are provided in this curriculum.)

Next, the leader invites the circle participants to voluntarily share their responses to the topic, one at a time. No one is forced to share, but everyone is given an opportunity to share while all the other circle members listen attentively. The circle participants tell the group about themselves, their personal experiences, thoughts, feelings, hopes and dreams as they relate to the topic. Most of the circle time is devoted to this sharing phase because of its central importance.

During this time, the leader assumes a dual role—that of leader and participant. The leader makes sure that everyone who wishes to speak is given the opportunity while simultaneously enforcing the rules as necessary. The leader also takes a turn to speak if he or she wishes.

After everyone who wants to share has done so, the leader introduces the next phase of the Sharing Circle by asking several discussion questions. This phase represents a transition to the intellectual mode and allows participants to reflect on and express learnings gained from the sharing phase and encourages participants to combine cognitive abilities and emotional experiencing. It's in this phase that participants are able to crystallize learnings and to understand the relevance of the discussion to their daily lives. (Discussion questions for each topic are provided in this curriculum.)

When the students have finished discussing their responses to the questions and the session has reached a natural closure, the leader ends the session. The leader thanks the students for being part of the Sharing Circle and states that it is over.

What follows is a more detailed look at the process of leading a Sharing Circle.

Steps for Leading a Sharing Circle

1. Welcome Sharing Circle members
2. Review the Sharing Circle rules*
3. Introduce the topic
4. Sharing by circle members
5. Ask discussion questions
6. Close the circle

*optional after the first few sessions

1. Welcome Sharing Circle members

As you sit down with the students in a Sharing Circle group, remember that you are not teaching a lesson. You are facilitating a group of people. Establish a positive atmosphere. In a relaxed manner, address each student by name, using eye contact and conveying warmth. An attitude of seriousness blended with enthusiasm will let the students know that this Sharing Circle group is an important learning experience—an activity that can be interesting and meaningful.

2. *Review the Sharing Circle rules*

At the beginning of the first Sharing Circle, and at appropriate intervals thereafter, go over the rules for the circle. They are:

Sharing Circle Rules

- Everyone gets a turn to share, including the leader.
- You can skip your turn if you wish.
- Listen to the person who is sharing.
- There are no interruptions, probing, put-downs, or gossip.
- Share the time equally.

From this point on, demonstrate to the students that you expect them to remember and abide by the ground rules. Convey that you think well of them and know they are fully capable of responsible behavior. Let them know that by coming to the Sharing Circle they are making a commitment to listen and show acceptance and respect for the other students and you. It is helpful to write the rules on chart paper and keep them on display for the benefit of each Sharing Circle session.

3. *Introduce the topic*

State the topic, and then in your own words, elaborate and provide examples as each lesson in this book suggests. The introduction or elaboration of the topic is designed to get students focused and thinking about how they will respond to the topic. By providing more than just the mere statement of the topic, the elaboration gives students a few moments to expand their thinking and to make a personal connection to the topic at hand. Add clarifying statements of your own that will help the students understand the topic. Answer questions about the topic, and emphasize that there are no "right" responses. Finally, restate the topic, opening the session to responses (theirs and yours). Sometimes taking your turn first helps the students understand the aim of the topic. The introductions, as written in this book, are provided to give you some general ideas for opening the Sharing Circle. It's important that you adjust and modify the introduction and elaboration to suit the ages, abilities, levels, cultural/ethnic backgrounds and interests of your students.

4. Sharing by circle members

The most important point to remember is this: The purpose of these Sharing Circles is to give students an opportunity to express themselves and be accepted for the experiences, thoughts, and feelings they share. Avoid taking the action away from the students. They are the stars!

5. Ask discussion questions

Responding to discussion questions is the cognitive portion of the process. During this phase, the leader asks thought-provoking questions to stimulate free discussion and higher-level thinking. Each Sharing Circle lesson in this book concludes with several discussion questions. At times, you may want to formulate questions that are more appropriate to the level of understanding in your students— or to what was actually shared in the circle. If you wish to make connections between the topic and your content area, ask questions that will accomplish that objective and allow the answering of the discussion questions to extend longer. We have left a space on each page for you to note significant other questions that you create and find effective.

6. Close the circle

The ideal time to end a Sharing Circle is when the discussion question phase reaches natural closure. Sincerely thank everyone for being part of the circle. Don't thank specific students for speaking, as doing so might convey the impression that speaking is more appreciated than mere listening. Then close the group by saying, "This Sharing Circle is over," or "OK, that ends our circle."

More about Sharing Circle Steps and Rules

The next few paragraphs offer further clarification concerning leadership of Sharing Circles.

Who gets to talk? Everyone. The importance of acceptance cannot be overly stressed. In one way or another practically every ground rule says one thing: accept one another. When you model acceptance of students, they will learn how to be accepting. Each individual in the group is important and deserves a turn to speak if he or she wishes to take it. Equal opportunity to become involved should be given to everyone in the Sharing Circle.

Members should be reinforced equally for their contributions. There are many reasons why a leader may become more enthused over what one student shares than another. The response may be more on target, reflect more depth, be more entertaining, be philosophically more in keeping with one's own point of view, and so on. However, students need to be given equal recognition for their contributions, even if the contribution is to listen silently throughout the session.

In most of the Sharing Circles, plan to take a turn and address the topic, too. Students usually appreciate it very much and learn a great deal when their teachers, counselors, and other adults are willing to tell about their own experiences, thoughts, and feelings. In this way you let your students know that you acknowledge your own humanness.

Does everyone have to take a turn? No. Students may choose to skip their turns. If the circle becomes a pressure situation in which the members are coerced in any way to speak, it will become an unsafe place where participants are not comfortable. Meaningful discussion is unlikely in such an atmosphere. By allowing students to make this choice, you are showing them that you accept their right to remain silent if that is what they choose to do.

As you begin the circle, it's important to remember that it's not a problem if one or more students decline to speak. If you are imperturbable and accepting when this happens, you let them know you are offering them an opportunity to experience something you think is valuable, or at least worth a try, and not attempting to force-feed them. You as a leader should not feel compelled to share a personal experience in every session, either. However, if you decline to speak in most of the sessions, this may have an inhibiting effect on the students' willingness to share.

A word should also be said about how this ground rule has sometimes been carried to extremes. Sometimes leaders have bent over backwards to let students know they don't have to take a turn. This seeming lack of enthusiasm on the part of the leader has caused reticence in the students. In order to avoid this outcome, don't project any personal insecurity as you lead the session. Be confident in your proven ability to work with students. Expect something to happen and it will.

Some leaders ask the participants to raise their hands when they wish to speak, while others simply allow free verbal sharing without soliciting the leader's permission first. Choose the procedure that works best for you, but do not call on anyone unless you can see signs of readiness. And do not merely go around the circle.

Some leaders have reported that their first group fell flat—that no one, or just one or two students, had anything to say. But they continued to have groups, and at a certain point everything changed. Thereafter, the students had a great deal to say that these leaders considered worth waiting for. It appears that in these cases the leaders' acceptance of the right to skip turns was a key factor. In time most students will contribute verbally when they have something they want to say, and when they are assured there is no pressure to do so.

Sometimes a silence occurs during a session. Don't feel you have to jump in every time someone stops talking. During silences students have an opportunity to think about what they would like to share or to contemplate an important idea they've heard. A general rule of thumb is to allow silence to the point that you observe group discomfort. At that point move on. Do not switch to another topic. To do so implies you will not be satisfied until the students speak. If you change to another topic, you are telling them you didn't really mean it when you said they didn't have to take a turn if they didn't want to.

If you are bothered about students who attend a number of sessions and still do not share verbally, reevaluate what you consider to be involvement. Participation does not necessarily mean talking. Students who do not speak are listening and learning.

How can I encourage effective listening? The Sharing Circle is a time (and place) for students and leaders to strengthen the habit of listening by doing it over and over again. No one was born knowing how to listen effectively to others. It is a skill like any other that gets better as it is practiced. In the immediacy of the Sharing Circle the members become keenly aware of the necessity to listen, and most students respond by expecting it of one another.

In these Sharing Circles, listening is defined as the respectful focusing of attention on individual speakers. It includes eye contact with the speaker and open body posture. It eschews interruptions of any kind. When you lead a circle, listen and encourage listening in the students by (1) focusing your attention on the person who is speaking, (2) being receptive to what the speaker is saying (not mentally planning your next remark), and (3) recognizing the speaker when she finishes speaking, either verbally ("Thanks, Shirley") or nonverbally (a nod and a smile).

To encourage effective listening in the students, reinforce them by letting them know you have noticed they were listening to each other and you appreciate it.

How can I ensure the students get equal time? When group members share the time equally, they demonstrate their acceptance of the notion that everyone's contribution is of equal importance. It is not uncommon to have at least one dominator in a group. This person is usually totally unaware that by continuing to talk he or she is taking time from others who are less assertive. An important social skill is knowing how you affect others in a group and when dominating a group is inappropriate behavior.

Be very clear with the students about the purpose of this ground rule. Tell them at the outset how much time there is. When it is your turn, always limit your own contribution. If someone goes on and on, do intervene (dominators need to know what they are doing), but do so as gently and respectfully as you can.

What are some examples of put-downs? Put-downs convey the message, "You are not okay as you are." Some put-downs are deliberate, but many are made unknowingly. Both kinds are undesirable in a Sharing Circle because they destroy the atmosphere of acceptance and disrupt the flow of sharing and discussion. Typical put-downs include:

- over questioning.
- statements that have the effect of teaching or preaching
- advice giving
- one-upsmanship
- criticism, disapproval, or objections
- sarcasm
- statements or questions of disbelief

How can I deal with put-downs? There are two major ways for dealing with put-downs: preventing them from occurring and intervening when they do.

Going over the rules with the students at the beginning of each Sharing Circle, particularly in the earliest sessions, is a helpful preventive technique. Another is to reinforce the students when they adhere to the rule. Be sure to use non patronizing, non evaluative language.

Unacceptable behavior should be stopped the moment it is recognized by the leader. When you become aware that a put-down is occurring, do whatever you ordinarily do to stop destructive behavior. If one student gives another an unasked-for bit of advice, say for example, "Jane, please give Alicia a chance to tell her story." To a student who interrupts say, "Ed, it's Sally's turn." In most cases the fewer words, the better—students automatically tune out messages delivered as lectures.

Sometimes students disrupt the group by starting a private conversation with the person next to them. Touch the offender on the arm or shoulder while continuing to give eye contact to the student who is speaking. If you can't reach the offender, simply remind him or her of the rule about listening.

If students persist in putting others down or disrupt the circle, ask to see them at another time and hold a brief one-to-one conference, urging them to follow the rules. Suggest that they reconsider their membership in the group. Make it clear that if they don't intend to honor the rules, they are not to come to the group.

How can I keep students from gossiping? Periodically remind students that using names and sharing embarrassing information in a Sharing Circle is not acceptable. Urge the students to relate personally to one another, but not to tell intimate details of their lives.

What should the leader do during the discussion question phase? Conduct this part of the process as an open forum, giving students the opportunity to discuss a variety of ideas and accept those that make sense to them. Don't impose your opinions on the students, or allow the students to impose theirs on one another. Ask open-ended questions, encourage higher-level thinking, contribute your own ideas when appropriate, and act as a facilitator.

In Conclusion: The Two Most Important Things to Remember

No matter what happens in a Sharing Circle session, the following two elements are the most critical:

1. Everyone gets a turn.
2. Everyone who takes a turn gets listened to with respect.

What does it mean to get a turn? Imagine a pie divided into as many pieces as there are people in the group. Telling the students that everyone gets a turn, whether they want to take it or not, is like telling them that each one gets a piece of the pie. Some students may not want their piece right away, but they know it's there to take when they do want it. As the teacher or counselor, you must protect this shared ownership. Getting a turn not only represents a chance to talk, it is an assurance that every member of the group has a "space" that no one else will violate.

When students take their turn, they will be listened to. There will be no attempt by anyone to manipulate what a student is offering. That is, the student will not be probed, interrupted, interpreted, analyzed, put-down, joked-at, advised, preached to, and so on. To "listen to" is to respectfully focus attention on the speaker and to let the speaker know that you have heard what he or she has said.

In the final analysis, the only way that a Sharing Circle can be evaluated is against these two criteria. Thus, if only two students choose to speak, but are listened to—even if they don't say very "deep" or "meaningful" things—the discussion group can be considered a success.

I Told the Truth and Was Glad

Purpose:

To help students develop an awareness of the consequences of dishonesty, and to encourage truthfulness.

Character Traits:

Honesty, Trustworthiness, Responsibility, Ethical Decision Making, Integrity

Introducing the Topic:

In your own words, say to the students: *Today's topic is, "I Told the Truth and Was Glad." Do you remember a time when you told the truth and were happy that you did? Maybe you were going to lie because that would have been easier, but you decided to tell the truth. Perhaps you spilled something on the sofa, or broke something, and didn't tell anyone at first, but admitted that you did it when an adult asked. Did you feel relieved after being honest, even if it meant paying for your mistake in some way? Maybe you saw a classmate stealing money from someone's desk and when the teacher asked if anyone knew what happened to the money you told the truth. Or maybe after lying about something, you felt bad, so you admitted your lie and told the truth. Think of a time when you told the truth and were glad that you did, even if it was hard to do. The topic is, "I Told the Truth and Was Glad."*

Discussion Questions:

— *Why is it important to tell the truth even when it is difficult?*
— *How do you feel about yourself when you lie? ...when you are truthful?*
— *How will telling the truth now make your life better when you are an adult?*

Your Questions:

A Hero Or Heroine I Admire

Purpose:

To encourage the students to identify people they greatly admire, and to describe admirable qualities in those people.

Character Traits:

Honesty, Determination, Responsibility, Trustworthiness, Courage, Integrity, Compassion

Introducing the Topic:

In your own words, say to the students: *Our topic for this circle is, "A Hero Or Heroine I Admire." As you look back at the people you've read and heard about who have done admirable and courageous things, which one stands out in your mind? Maybe you are impressed by a hero or heroine who stood up for people's rights, or one who had the courage to say or do things that no one else would do. Perhaps your hero risked her life to save a child, or devoted his life to discovering a cure for some disease. Your chosen hero or heroine may be one of the people you've studied in school, or it could be someone you know — a relative or friend whom you greatly admire. Give it some thought. Tell us who your hero or heroine is and what that person did to earn your admiration. Our topic is, "A Hero or Heroine I Admire."*

Discussion Questions:

— *How are our heroes alike? How are they different?*
— *Why do people have heroes and heroines?*
— *What do heroes and heroines teach us?*
— *What character traits does your hero or heroine demonstrate that you admire?*

Your Questions:

I Respected Myself for Something I Did

Purpose:

To identify specific behaviors that earn the respect of self and others.

Character Traits:

Respect, Self Management

Introducing the Topic:

In your own words, say to the students: *Today we're going to talk about respect — what it is and why people appreciate being treated respectfully. You have probably noticed that certain actions are respectful and that some people are particularly deserving of respect because they have done things we admire.*

Our topic for this session is, "I Respected Myself for Something I Did." This is a very important topic because it reminds us that the person who most needs our respect is ourself. Sometimes we do things that make us feel particularly proud. Think of a time when you did something you were very pleased with. Maybe you helped someone who needed and wanted your help, or perhaps you were tempted to do something that might have hurt someone, like gossiping or telling a secret, but you stopped yourself. Maybe you told the truth, even though it was hard, or refused to go along when other kids did something wrong. Think about it for a few moments. The topic is, "I Respected Myself for Something I Did."

Discussion Questions:

— What kinds of actions cause self-respect?
— Why is it important to respect yourself?
— If you don't respect yourself, is it likely that other people will respect you? Why or why not?

Your Questions

A Time I Showed Someone That I Cared

Purpose:

To acknowledge, validate, and support caring behaviors.

Character Traits:

Caring, Responsibility, Compassion

Introducing the Topic:

In your own words, say to the students: *Our topic today is, "A Time I Showed Someone That I Cared." We are all affected by people who care about us. And we have the ability to influence how others feel as well. Think of a time when you showed someone that you cared and it made the person feel good. Have you ever tried to cheer up a friend who was feeling badly? Perhaps you helped a younger brother with his homework or a little sister tie her shoes. Maybe when your parent was tired from working all day, you helped prepare dinner. Or maybe you told a friend that you understood how he or she felt because you'd felt that same way. How did the person react to your caring behavior? How did you feel about what you did? Think of the many times you have shown someone that you cared, and share one example with us. Our topic is, "A Time I Showed Someone That I Cared."*

Discussion Questions:

— *How do we affect the world we live in when we show people that we care about them?*
— *Why is it important for us to see ourselves as caring people?*
— *How do we learn to be caring people?*
— *How do you feel about yourself when you show care and concern for others? How do others feel about you?*

Your Questions:

What It Means to Live By the Golden Rule

Purpose:

To help students learn to judge the effects of their actions; to understand and apply the Golden Rule.

Character Traits:

Open Mindedness, Tolerance, Empathy, Respect, Caring, Fairness, Compassion

Introducing the Topic:

In your own words, say to the students: *Our topic today is one that calls for an opinion, so you'll want to think it through carefully. It is, "What It Means to Live By the Golden Rule." The Golden Rule says "Do unto others what you would have them do unto you." or "Treat others like you want to be treated." If you always followed that rule, what would your life be like? What effect would the Golden Rule have on your behavior?*

How would you act at home toward your family? How would you treat people here at school? How would the Golden Rule affect the things you say to and about others? Imagine yourself following this rule all the time, and tell us what you think it would be like. The topic is, "What It Means to Live By the Golden Rule."

Discussion Questions:

— *How difficult would it be to follow the Golden Rule all the time? How would it feel?*
— *Does living by the Golden Rule affect your thoughts, or just your actions?*
— *What would life be like if everyone followed the Golden Rule at home? ...at school? ...in the community? ...in the world?*

Your Questions:

How I Show That I'm a Good School Citizen

Purpose:

To identify and discuss specific behaviors that comprise proactive, responsible citizenship.

Character Traits:

Citizenship, Responsibility, Self Discipline, Self Management, Positive Attitude

Introducing the Topic:

In your own words, say to the students: *We have two major jobs to do at school. One is to be a good student — to study and learn. The other is to be a contributing member of the school community — a good citizen. In this session, we're going to focus on the job of citizenship. Our topic is, "How I Show That I'm a Good School Citizen."*

Tell us one way in which you demonstrate that you are a good citizen here at school. Think about the things you do in class and on the playground that help the school community function well. Maybe you make a habit of always following the rules. Perhaps you volunteer for jobs in the classroom, like erasing the board, putting away materials and equipment, or tutoring other kids. Or maybe you participate in a school-wide volunteer group, such as the safety patrol, or the conflict mediation team. Do you always put your trash in a trash receptacle? Do you take home notices and bring back permission slips on time? Do you take part in special events, like assemblies, holiday celebrations, and open house? Think about it for a few moments. Being a good citizen involves many different kinds of attitudes and actions. Our topic is, "How I Show That I'm a Good School Citizen."

Discussion Questions:

— *Why is it important to be a good school citizen?*
— *How is being a good citizen of the school similar to being a good citizen of the community? How is it different?*
— *Is part of being a good citizen encouraging others to be good citizens? What are some examples?*

Your Questions:

A Rule We Have In My Family

Purpose:

This topic invites students to talk about the rules that they see in their own families and to discuss how these help to shape character.

Character Traits:

Citizenship, Responsibility, Self-Management

Introducing the Topic:

In your own words, say to the students: *The topic for today is, "A Rule We Have In My Family." Families like all other organizations have to establish rules. You are probably glad to have some family rules, but don't feel so good about others. Think about the rules in your family and describe one to us.*

Maybe your family has a rule that requires you to finish your chores before playing or going out with friends. Maybe homework must be completed before watching television, and no name-calling or fighting is allowed. Some families have rules about bedtime, having friends over when no adult is home, and maintaining a degree of cleanliness and order in each person's room. Think about the rules in your family and choose one to share. Our topic is, "A Rule We Have In My Family."

Discussion Questions:

— *How well do the rules work in your family?*
— *How would things be different if your family did not have these rules?*
— *If you have a family, what rules do you think you will establish?*
— *Why are rules important in any group or organization of people?*
— *What do you learn from having rules?*

Your Questions:

A Character Trait I Admire in Others

Purpose:

To help students identify admirable qualities and to explain how such qualities contribute to "good character."

Character Traits:

All positive traits discussed in this session

Introducing the Topic:

In your own words, say to the students: *We can all identify many important character traits — qualities in ourselves and others that we value, such as honesty, tolerance, trustworthiness, caring, forgiveness, respectfulness, responsibility, and fairness. In this session, we're going to think of one quality that we particularly value. Our topic is, "A Character Trait I Admire in Others."*

One way to do this is to think of one or two people whom you really like and respect. Then ask yourself what character trait really stands out in each of these people. You might decide that the strongest character trait they have is honesty. Perhaps they are always truthful, never try to avoid responsibility for their actions by lying, and tell you exactly what they think so you never have to wonder. Maybe you admire people who show a lot of caring and concern for others, try to be helpful, and go out of their way to do thoughtful things. Or perhaps you admire people who accept responsibility without hesitation, who are leaders, and who are the first to act when something needs to be done. Think about it for a few moments. Our topic is, "A Character Trait I Admire in Others."

Discussion Questions:

— Why is it important to have good character?
— How are good character traits developed?
— What good qualities would you like people to recognize in you?
— What character traits would you like to change?

Your Questions:

Someone I Know Who Is an Accepting Person

Purpose:

This topic asks students to describe the positive qualities of people they know whose behavior is non-judgmental and non-evaluative, and to explore the positive feelings that accepting people inspire in them.

Character Traits:

Open-Mindedness, Fairness, Respect

Introducing the Topic:

In your own words, say to the students: *Our topic for today is, "Someone I Know Who Is an Accepting Person." One of the interesting things about knowing an accepting person is that you usually feel good when you are around him or her. Do you know why? An accepting person lets you be you. He or she accepts all the things you are — your strengths and your weaknesses — and doesn't judge, stereotype, or label you.*

Think of such a person in your life — someone who accepts you just the way you are. This person might be a parent, friend, teacher, brother or sister, doctor — anyone you know. What does this person do or say that causes you to feel accepted? How do you feel about this person? Take a minute to think about it. The topic is, "Someone I Know Who Is an Accepting Person."

Discussion Questions:

— What are some ways in which people show acceptance?
— How do you act when you are around a person who is non-judgmental?
— What is the opposite of accepting?
— How do you act when you are around someone who is unaccepting?
— Why is accepting differences in others important?

Your Questions:

Someone Who Trusts Me

Purpose:

This topic asks students to describe the positive feelings they experience when they earn another person's trust. In the process, they define trust and explain how it develops between people.

Character Traits:

Trustworthiness, Responsibility, Self-Discipline, Self-Management

Introducing the Topic:

In your own words, say to the students: *Today, we are going to discuss the subject of trust. Our topic is, "Someone Who Trusts Me." Think of a person who trusts you, and tell us how your earned that trust. The person could be a parent, friend, relative, or teacher.*

Did this person always trust you, or did you have to prove that you were trustworthy? Maybe you showed that you could be trusted to take care of a younger brother or sister. Perhaps you showed your parent that you could be trusted to go places with friends and always be home on time. Or you might have earned the trust of a friend or parent by always telling the truth, even when it might get you in trouble. How do you feel knowing that you are trusted by this person? How does it affect your relationships with other people? Take a minute to think about it, and then let's talk about, "Someone Who Trusts Me."

Discussion Questions:

— What is trust?
— How do you learn to trust another person?
— Is trust always mutual? Why or why not?
— What kinds of things can destroy trust?
— Why is trust important in relationships?

Your Questions:

When Someone Criticized Me

Purpose:

This topic invites students to examine an incident in which they were criticized, to distinguish between helpful and hurtful criticism, and to talk about various ways in which criticism affects people.

Character Traits:

Positive Attitude, Caring, Respect, Responsibility

Introducing the Topic:

In your own words, say to the students: *In this session, we are going to focus on the effects of criticism. The topic is, "When Someone Criticized Me." Think of a time when someone criticized you, and try to recall how you felt when it happened. Also, think about the situation and what was going on that brought about the criticism. Did you get a poor report card, fail to keep a promise, or say something thoughtless? Or did the criticism have to do with your clothes, hairstyle, or some other aspect of your appearance?*

How did you feel about the criticism? Perhaps you felt it was unjustified or too harsh — not helpful at all. Or maybe you gained somehow because of the criticism. Were the intentions of the person offering the criticism positive, or was this person being picky or cruel? Take a minute to think about it, and if you will, tell us about a time like this in your life. The topic is, "When Someone Criticized Me."

Discussion Questions:

— *What methods of offering suggestions or criticism tend to be most effective? ...least effective?*
— *What is meant by the term constructive criticism?*
— *If you have trouble receiving criticism, how can you learn to handle it better?*
— *How does your attitude affect how you handle criticism?*
— *What did you learn from being criticized?*

Your Questions:

A Time I Kept My Promise

Purpose:

This topic allows students to explain the value of keeping promises, associate feelings with honesty, and associate honesty with the development of trust.

Character Traits:

Honesty, Responsibility, Trustworthiness, Self-Discipline, Integrity, Ethical Decision-Making

Introducing the Topic:

In your own words, say to the students: *Today's topic is, "A Time I Kept My Promise." Have you ever made a promise to someone and kept it? You said that you were going to do something, or not do something, and you followed through — even though it might have taken some hard work. Maybe you promised your dad that you would sweep the kitchen or patio after school and you did it. Perhaps you made a promise to a friend that you would go to his house on a Saturday to help with math homework and you went, even though you had to give up a more enjoyable activity. Maybe you promised your teacher that you would try harder to be quiet during study time, and by really working at it you succeeded. Or perhaps you promised not to do something, like not to fight with your sister or brother when the two of you were alone. How did you feel about keeping your word? Did anyone notice or acknowledge you for keeping your promise? Try to remember a time that you made a promise and kept it, and get ready to share it with the group. The topic is, "A Time I Kept My Promise."*

Discussion Questions:

— Why is it important to keep promises when we make them?
— How does it feel when someone makes a promise to you and keeps it? ...doesn't keep it?
— How does keeping, or not keeping, promises affect the willingness of others to trust you?

Your Questions:

One of the Nicest Things a Friend Ever Did for Me

Purpose:

This topic asks students to verbalize their feelings concerning a friend's welcome deed or gesture, and to explore qualities of positive friendships.

Character Traits:

Empathy, Generosity, Positive Attitude

Introducing the Topic:

In your own words, say to the students: *Today, we are going to talk about the kinds of things that friends do for each other. The topic is, "One of the Nicest Things a Friend Ever Did for Me."*

Think back over all of the things your friends have done for you and pick one incident that gives you particular warmth and pleasure. Perhaps your friend planned ahead of time, throwing you a birthday party or taking you on a special outing, or maybe your friend acted spontaneously by suddenly complementing you or pledging to always be friends. Has a friend ever loaned you a favorite article of clothing or musical recording, or sat with you for hours while you waited for some important news? Has a friend ever helped you get your chores done so you could both go to movie? Tell us what your friend did and how you felt about it. The topic is, "One of the Nicest Things a Friend Ever Did for Me."

Discussion Questions:

— How did your friend seem to feel about the thing he or she did?
— How did you express your appreciation to your friend?
— Why are friendships so important in our lives?
— Who benefits when friends do nice things for each other?
— Why is it important to express appreciation to someone who does something nice for you?

Your Questions:

Someone Helped Me When I Needed and Wanted Help

Purpose:

This topic asks students to describe an incident in which they received help that was both necessary and desired. In the process, they explore feelings and behaviors associated with receiving and giving help.

Character Traits:

Empathy, Responsibility, Caring

Introducing the Topic:

In your own words, say to the students: *Our discussion topic for this session is, "Someone Helped Me When I Needed and Wanted Help." Often, though we need help and ask for it, we don't get it for some reason. On the other hand, sometimes we don't want help, but get it anyway, whether we like it or not. But every once in awhile, we're lucky enough to get the help that we both need and want.*

Help can take many forms. Maybe someone brought you a part for a broken bike, medicine when you were sick in bed, or notes from a class that you missed. The help might have been emotionally supportive, like love from a person who really cared about you, or a pat on the shoulder when you were feeling down or lonely. Think back for a moment. The topic is, "Someone Helped Me When I Needed and Wanted Help."

Discussion Questions:

— *How did you feel when you received the help you needed and wanted?*
— *How do you think the person who helped you felt?*
— *How can you tell when a person not only desires help, but truly needs it?*

Your Questions:

Something I'm Learning Now That Is Difficult

Purpose:

This topic encourages students to examine a learning problem that they are having, to realize that learning problems are normal and universally experienced, and to explore remedies for learning problems.

Character Traits:

Perseverance, Self-Discipline

Introducing the Topic:

In your own words, say to the students: *Today, we are going to talk about times when learning is tough — and it is for all of us now and then. Our topic is, "Something I'm Learning Now That Is Difficult." Is there anything you are learning at this time, either here at school or somewhere else, that is hard for you? If so, please tell us what it is and what makes it difficult. Maybe you are studying a foreign language, and remembering all of the vocabulary and grammar is tough. Perhaps you are having difficulty with math, writing, or physical education. Or maybe the thing that is difficult for you is learning to be on time, make new friends, or control your temper. Practically everything we do involves learning, so difficult learning can occur in almost any area. Think about it for a moment. The topic is, "Something I'm Learning Now That Is Difficult."*

Discussion Questions:

— *What similarities did you notice in the kinds of difficulties we are having?*
— *What can you do to help yourself learn more easily in the area you mentioned?*
— *What do you think the benefit will be of "sticking to it," and learning this difficult thing well?*

Your Questions:

A Way I Earned Something and What I Did With It

Purpose:

This topic asks students to describe a way in which they earned money, or another reward, and to examine the connection between effort and reward.

Character Traits:

Responsibility, Self-Discipline, Determination

Introducing the Topic:

In your own words, say to the students: *Today let's talk about, "A Way I Earned Something and What I Did With It." Think about a time when you completed some kind of work and earned something for it (not necessarily money). Maybe you did some work around your home and earned the privilege of a weekend completely free of chores, and you spent most of your free weekend at a friend's house. Perhaps you earned extra money baby-sitting or taking care of a neighbor's pet, and spent the money at a theme park or bought some new clothes. Was the work you did your idea, or did someone else ask you to do it? How did you feel after you earned something for your efforts? Were you motivated to do it again? Give it some thought. The topic is, "A Way I Earned Something and What I Did With It."*

Discussion Questions:

— *If you knew in advance that you were going to be rewarded for your efforts, how did that influence your willingness to make the effort?*
— *Should we always be rewarded in some way for our efforts? Why or why not?*
— *How do you feel when you put a lot of effort into something and receive no reward at all, not even a thank you?*
— *What ideas did you get from this session about ways to earn money, or other things?*

Your Questions:

A Responsible Habit I've Developed

Purpose:

The topic invites students to describe and take credit for responsible behaviors and to realize that responsible habits are developed through repeated practice.

Character Traits:

Responsibility, All positive character traits discussed in this session

Introducing the Topic:

In your own words, say to the students: *No matter how responsible we already are, we can always learn more about this important value. It's also important to give ourselves credit for the responsible things we do on a regular basis. Our topic for this sharing circle is, "A Responsible Habit I've Developed."*

When we do something again and again it becomes a habit. That's how some of our responsible actions become habits. We do them so often we don't even think about them anymore. Do you have any habits like that? Maybe you brush your teeth every day without being reminded, put your dirty clothes in a hamper as soon as you take them off, or pick up things you see lying around the house. Perhaps you feed and exercise a pet regularly, make your bed as soon as you get up in the morning, or check every weekend to see if you can do anything to assist an elderly neighbor. Or maybe you always finish your homework before watching TV, or your yard chores before going off to play on Saturday. Think it over and tell us about a responsible action that you do regularly. Our topic is, "A Responsible Habit I've Developed."

Discussion Questions:

— *How does having a responsible habit make you feel about yourself?*
— *Can you simply decide to develop a habit and then do it? Why or why not?*
— *How are habits developed?*
— *What responsible habits did you hear about today that you would like to develop, too?*

Your Questions:

A Time I Was Afraid, But I Did It Anyway

Purpose:

This topic invites students to recall an incident in which they were courageous, took a risk, or simply persisted. In the process, they describe some of the challenges of following a courageous path.

Character Traits:

Perserverence, Self-Discipline, Courage

Introducing the Topic:

In your own words, say to the students: *Our topic for today is, "A Time I Was Afraid, But I Did It Anyway." Can you think of a time when you hesitated to do something, but then decided to take a risk and do it? Maybe you hesitated to apply for a job, ask someone to be your friend, or go to a meeting where you didn't know anyone. Perhaps you needed to summon your courage to run for office, try out for a team, or see your counselor about a problem. Did anyone help you to find the courage you needed, or did you do it on your own? Think about it for a moment. The topic is, "A Time I Was Afraid, But I Did It Anyway."*

Discussion Questions:

— *How do you feel now about the incident you shared?*
— *Why is it hard to be courageous at times?*
— *Are there times when the most courageous thing to do is nothing? Give an example.*

Your Questions:

I Stood Up for Something I Strongly Believe In

Purpose:

To describe incidents that demonstrate personal integrity; to explain the connection between integrity and trustworthiness.

Character Traits:

Honesty, Determination, Responsibility, Trustworthiness, Self Discipline, Courage, Ethical Decision Making, Integrity

Introducing the Topic:

In your own words, say to the students: *Today's topic is, "I Stood Up for Something I Strongly Believe In." Most of us have experienced at least once the necessity to take a stand concerning something. Standing up for a belief can be difficult, especially if friends or family do not agree with us. Even when they do agree, it is not necessarily easy to state our beliefs publicly. Think of a time when this happened to you.*

Maybe you saw others doing something that you felt was wrong, and you confronted them. Perhaps you were involved in a discussion about a controversial subject, and you stated your views, even though they were unpopular. You may remember being nervous and worrying about what might happen or what someone would think. Or you may have felt very sure of yourself. Perhaps when you look back on the occasion, you recall a sense of pride, accomplishment, or even daring. If the outcome was different from what you wanted, tell us what you learned from the experience. Remember, don't mention any names. The topic is, "I Stood Up for Something I Strongly Believe In."

Discussion Questions:

— *As you look back on the situation you shared, how do you feel about it right now?*
— *Why is it sometimes hard to stand up for your beliefs?*
— *What are the risks and benefits of taking a stand?*
— *What are some ills in our society that people need to take a stand against?*
— *How do your values help you take a strong stand?*

Your Questions:

How I Helped Someone Who Was Having a Problem

Purpose:

In this discussion, the students describe an incident in which they helped another person. In the process, they distinguish between appropriate and inappropriate ways of offering help.

Character Traits:

Generosity, Empathy

Introducing the Topic:

In your own words, say to the students: *Our topic for today is, "How I Helped Someone Who Was Having a Problem." Think of a time when you were a real help to someone who was having difficulty with something. Think about what you did or said that assisted this person. Maybe you helped a classmate solve a tough math problem or get started on a complicated assignment. Perhaps you assisted a person with a disability to get through a narrow aisle or down a steep ramp. Or you might have offered to listen so a friend could talk through a personal problem or difficult decision. Give it some thought. Tell us what happened and how you felt. The topic is, "How I Helped Someone Who Was Having a Problem."*

Discussion Questions:

— *When you help someone who needs and wants help, how do you generally feel about yourself?*
— *Is it a good idea to always jump in and help a person who is having a problem? Why or why not?*
— *How can you find out if help is both needed and wanted?*

Your Questions:

It Was Hard to Say No, But I Did

Purpose:

This topic asks students to describe a time when they were assertive against difficult odds, standing up for their own convictions in the face of pressure.

Character Traits:

Self-Control, Self-Discipline, Empathy, Courage, Determination

Introducing the Topic:

In your own words, say to the students: *Today we're going to talk about a time when we were assertive — when we stood up for our own wants and feelings. Our topic is, "It Was Hard to Say No, But I Did."*

Often we go along with what other people want us to do or believe because it seems like the easiest, most acceptable thing to do. There are times, however, when our convictions tell us to follow a different course. Can you think of a time when you stood up for your own beliefs and feelings? Maybe a close friend asked you to do something, and though you hated to disappoint him or her, you found the courage to say no. Perhaps you were tempted to have a second helping of dessert, but summoned the willpower to say no. Or maybe someone asked you to tell a secret, and you were really tempted to talk, but at the last second stopped yourself. Think it over for a minute and then, if you will, tell us about a time like this in your life. The topic is, "It Was Hard to Say No, But I Did."

Discussion Questions:

— How can you say no effectively, without hurting the other person's feelings?
— In what kinds of situations is it hardest to be assertive?
— How can learning to be assertive help you throughout your life?
— How do your values help you determine the things you need to say no to?

Your Questions:

What I Think Good Communication Is

Purpose:

This topic challenges students to describe the ingredients of effective communication. In the process they examine the important role communication plays in relationships.

Character Traits:

Open-Mindedness, Fairness, Respect

Introducing the Topic:

In your own words, say to the students: *Our topic for this circle session is, "What I Think Good Communication Is." Almost all of the contact we have with other people involves communicating in one way or another. Sometimes this communication is in writing and other times it involves speaking and listening. In addition, a good deal of our communication involves body language. We call this* nonverbal *communication. Think about the things you must do to be a good communicator, and tell us what you think is involved in truly good communication. If you like, you may describe a specific example of good communication; for example, an exchange that you had with a friend or family member that worked out very well. When you are ready, we can begin. The topic is, "What I Think Good Communication Is."*

Discussion Questions:

— What are some of the results of good communication?
— What can happen when communication is NOT good?
— How do you feel when communication between you and another person is good? ...is poor?
— How does accepting someone's feelings show respect for that person?

Your Questions:

What I Value Most in a Friend

Purpose:

This topic allows students to explore the many qualities and traits that are the vital ingredients of friendships.

Character Traits:

All positive character traits discussed in this session

Introducing the Topic:

In your own words, say to the students: *Good friends can be and do many things for each other. I would like you to decide what some of those things are for today's circle topic, "What I Value Most in a Friend."*

What do you and your friends say and do to make your friendships work, and to make them special? What qualities do you think are important in a friend? Do you value honesty? ...loyalty? ...listening? ...common interests? ...having time to be together? Think about it for a moment and, when you are ready, our topic is, "What I Value Most in a Friend."

Discussion Questions:

— *What are some of the main qualities that we value in friends?*
— *How do you feel about your friend when he or she does or says something that you think is valuable to the friendship?*
— *If you want your friends to behave in the ways we talked about, would be wise for you to do the same things? Why?*

Your Questions:

What I Do When the Going Gets Tough

Purpose:

This topic asks students to talk about successful methods they've developed for handling stressful situations in their lives.

Character Traits:

Positive Attitude, Self-Control, Self-Discipline

Introducing the Topic:

In your own words, say to the students: *Our topic for this session is, "What I Do When the Going Gets Tough." Most of us have ways to make ourselves feel better when we are stressed. What's one of your ways? What do you do to help yourself when you feel angry, worried, tense, or nervous? Maybe you talk to one of your parents or to a friend about what's bothering you. Or perhaps you take a long walk or bike ride. Spending time alone with your pet may make you feel better. Or perhaps you do something to take your mind off the stressful situation—like watching TV, going to a movie, or reading a book. Tell us what you do, and how you feel when you do it. Let's think it over for a few moments. The topic is, "What I Do When the Going Gets Tough."*

Discussion Questions:

— Why is it important to find positive ways to handle difficult situations?
— What are some negative ways in which people try to handle stress?
— Do you think fewer people would use alcohol and drugs if they knew how to handle stress in more positive ways?
— What new methods of handling stressful situations did you learn from this discussion?

Your Questions:

An Ability or Talent I'm Proud Of

Purpose:

This topic invites every student to describe one ability or talent they possess. Students demonstrate appreciation for the abilities of others, and discuss the importance of acknowledging their own strengths and abilities.

Character Traits:

Positive Attitude, Self-Discipline, Confidence, Enthusiasm, Thankfulness

Introducing the Topic:

In your own words, say to the students: *This is going to be an unusual circle session because we are going to encourage each other to do something most people don't do very often. We're going to take credit for things we're good at. Most of the time people are modest, but today we will ignore any rules of modesty we've learned, which will probably do us good. The topic is, "An Ability or Talent I'm Proud Of."*

It's obvious that everyone has strengths and weaknesses. No one is good at everything and no one is poor at everything. Think for a minute about those things at which you are just naturally good. Think about your special skills. Maybe you excel in an academic area like Math, Science, or English. Or perhaps you have an athletic skill you're proud of. Maybe you have artistic talents, or are good at making things with your hands. You might have inherited your abilities from your parents, or you may be the only one in your family who has them. Think it over for a few moments. The topic is, "An Ability or Talent I'm Proud Of."

Discussion Questions:

— *How did you feel telling us about your abilities and talents? Did it feel a bit like bragging?*
— *What benefits do we get from talking about our strengths and abilities?*
— *How did you feel about each other during this session?*
— *How did you develop your strengths and abilities?*

Your Questions:

Something I Enjoy Doing Because It Gives Me a Feeling of Accomplishment

Purpose:

This topic asks students to link an activity they enjoy to the sense of accomplishment it produces. Students acknowledge some of their own abilities and recognize how cultivating those abilities can lead to personal rewards.

Character Traits:

Perseverance, Self-Discipline, Positive Attitude, Confidence

Introducing the Topic:

In your own words, say to the students: *Today we're going to discuss things we are good at. The topic is, "Something I Enjoy Doing Because It Gives Me a Feeling of Accomplishment." Notice that you are asked to brag a little here, and that's OK. You aren't boasting, and you are not comparing yourself to others or putting anyone else down. You are just telling about something you can do that you're proud of. So think about one thing you like to do that gives you a good feeling. This can be something you enjoy doing at school or away from school. It can be something you've only done once, or an activity you engage in frequently. Think about it for a minute. The topic is, "Something I Enjoy Doing Because It Gives Me A Feeling of Accomplishment."*

Discussion Questions:

— What is it about the activity you shared that gives you such good feelings?
— How important is it to experience feelings of accomplishment?
— Did you learn anything new and interesting about anyone in this session?
— What did you learn about yourself?

Your Questions:

I Thought Over My Decision, and I Stuck to It

Purpose:

This topic asks students to describe a decision and the process they used to make it. The students also discuss the importance of identifying and evaluating alternatives when making decisions.

Character Traits:

Perseverance, Self-Control, Self-Discipline

Introducing the Topic:

In your own words, say to the students: *Today our topic is, "I Thought Over My Decision, and I Stuck to It." Try to recall a time when you had to make an important decision, perhaps a very tough one. Maybe your intuition told you what would be best right away. Or perhaps there was a lot of pressure on you to decide quickly. Later, however, you had a chance to think over the situation more carefully. Perhaps you started to see how difficult it was going to be to follow through. For example, maybe you decided to take two very tough classes at the same time, and later realized how much homework was involved. At that point, you considered changing your mind.*

You thought about alternatives — other choices you could make and how each choice might turn out. You probably considered how well each option would work and how it would affect other people, too. And after all the study and evaluation, you stuck to your original decision, even though that might have been difficult. Take a few minutes to consider the topic — "I Thought Over My Decision, and I Stuck to It."

Discussion Questions:

— How do you feel about your decision now?
— Is it possible to make good decisions based on intuition or a hunch? Why or why not?
— What can you do to verify that your intuition is correct?
— Why is it important to look at alternatives?
— How can you go about identifying alternatives? . . . evaluating the possible consequences of each alternative?

Your Questions:

When One Person Kept Blaming Another for Causing a Problem

Purpose:

This topic allows students to recognize how unproductive it can be to "pass the buck" or blame others for problems that need to be solved.

Character Traits:

Respect, Empathy, Open-Mindedness

Introducing the Topic:

In your own words, say to the students: *In today's session, we're going to talk about what can happen when we get caught up in the "blaming game." Our topic is, "When One Person Kept Blaming Another for Causing a Problem." Maybe you were involved or maybe you were just an observer, but what we're after today are situations in which it was important to one person to blame another for a problem. The focus in these situations was on who <u>caused</u> the problem, not on how to <u>solve</u> it. Common words in situations like this are, "You always..." or "You never..." If you decide to share, tell us about the problem and how one person kept blaming the other (or maybe they both did it to each other), without telling us who the people were. The topic is, "When One Person Kept Blaming Another for Causing a Problem."*

Discussion Questions:

— What good does blaming do?
— What harm can blaming do?
— How can we train ourselves to put our energies into problem solving instead of into anger, frustration, and blaming?

Your Questions:

I Got Blamed for Something I Didn't Do

Purpose:

This topic asks students to describe a situation in which they were wrongly accused, and helps them to identify effective ways of responding to false accusations.

Character Traits:

Fairness, Open-Mindedness, Self-Control, Respect

Introducing the Topic:

In your own words, say to the students: *Our circle session topic today is a challenging one. It's about one of the most distressing things that can happen to a person. The topic is, "I Got Blamed for Something I Didn't Do." Probably everyone has had this happen at least once and it can certainly be upsetting.*

So give it some thought. Maybe you denied having done the thing you were being blamed for, and your denial was accepted. Or perhaps you denied it, and the other people involved didn't believe you. Whatever happened, if you'd like to tell us about it, we'd appreciate hearing. Tell us what happened, and how you felt, but don't mention any names. Our topic is, "I Got Blamed for Something I Didn't Do."

Discussion Questions:

— Why is it so upsetting to be blamed for something you didn't do?
— How can you handle a situation in which you are wrongly blamed?
— What does this session teach us about blaming?

Your Questions:

A Time Someone Put Me Down, But I Handled It Well

Purpose:

This topic asks students to describe a potential conflict situation that they handled well, and to identify effective methods of self-control that can be used to avoid conflict.

Character Traits:

Self-Control, Self-Discipline, Forgiveness, Fairness, Respect

Introducing the Topic:

In your own words, say to the students: *Our topic for today is, "A Time Someone Put Me Down, But I Handled It Well." Think about a situation in which you were criticized, ridiculed, ignored, or in some other way diminished, but you managed to maintain your dignity and didn't let it upset you too much. Perhaps you broke something, or made a mistake, or behaved awkwardly, and even though your behavior was unintentional, someone put you down for it. What did the other person say or do? Were there other people present? How did you feel, and what did you do to control your reactions? Without mentioning any names, tell us about, "A Time Someone Put Me Down, But I Handled It Well."*

Discussion Questions:

— *How do you feel now about the person who put you down?*
— *What methods did we use to keep our cool in the face of the put-downs mentioned?*
— *When seemingly harmless put-downs turn into serious conflicts, what can we do?*

Your Questions:

How I Made Someone Feel Happy

Purpose:

This topic helps students identify behaviors that affect others in a positive way. At the same time, the students recognize that bringing happiness to others bolsters their own good feelings and self-esteem.

Character Traits:

Generosity, Empathy, Responsibility, Caring, Sociability, Positive Attitude, Self-Management

Introducing the Topic:

In your own words, say to the students: *Today we are going to talk about behaviors that create positive feelings in others. Our topic is, "How I Made Someone Feel Happy." Think about a time when you said or did something that made someone else feel good. It may have been something you thought about, planned and worked on for a long time, or you may have acted spontaneously—on the spur of the moment. Describe what you did to make the other person happy and how you felt knowing that you were the cause of his or her happiness. The topic is, "How I Made Someone Feel Happy."*

Discussion Questions:

— How can you tell when someone feels happy?
— What usually happens to your own feelings when you succeed in making another person feel happy?
— How does making another person happy affect your self-esteem?

Your Questions:

Someone I Learned To Trust

Purpose:

Students examine how trust develops between people, and think about feelings associated with trust and distrust. By examining group distrust (racial, political, etc.), students identify its causes.

Character Traits:

Empathy, Respect, Open-Mindedness, Forgiveness, Tolerance, Caring, Fairness, Sociability, Compassion

Introducing the Topic:

In your own words, say to the students: *The topic for today is, "Someone I Learned To Trust." When we trust someone, we usually like and respect them as well. But there are times when we like a person, yet aren't really sure that we can trust them. Have you ever felt this way about someone? Maybe the person reminded you of someone who couldn't be trusted, or belonged to a group that you'd heard bad things about. Whatever the reasons, you had to <u>learn</u> to trust the person, which probably took a little time. Without using any names, tell us about a time when you learned to trust someone after you'd known him or her for a while. Tell us how you felt about the person at first, and then what happened that caused trust to develop in the relationship. The topic is, "Someone I Learned To Trust."*

Discussion Questions:

— *What does it take to feel instant trust for another person?*
— *How does trust develop in a relationship?*
— *Why are members of one group often reluctant to trust members of a different group?*

Your Questions:

Something I Finished That I Had a Hard Time Starting

Purpose:

In this discussion, students describe how they completed an extremely difficult task. In the process they identify thoughts and attitudes that facilitate goal attainment.

Character Traits:

Positive Attitude, Perserverence, Self-Discipline

Introducing the Topic:

In your own words, say to the students: *Our circle session topic for today is, "Something I Finished That I Had a Hard Time Starting." Do you remember the story of "The Little Engine That Could?" You probably heard it as a child. It was about the little red engine that managed to chug its way over a high mountain because it was sure it could do it. We've all experienced times when we took on something that seemed much too big for us, or when someone gave us a pretty rough assignment or job. It looked so impossible at first that it was hard to get started.*

Think of a time like that in your life. Maybe you were given a homework assignment that seemed insurmountable. Or perhaps you were involved in a special project or event that was very involved and complex. Yet, regardless of how difficult it seemed at first, you finished it. Let's take a few moments to think it over. The topic is, "Something I Finished That I Had a Hard Time Starting."

Discussion Questions:

— How did your feelings change from the time you began the task till the time you completed it?
— What kind of attitude can help a person begin a difficult task?
— Sometimes tasks are easy to start but hard to finish. What attitudes help out in these situations?

Your Questions:

A Time I Was Involved in a Misunderstanding

Purpose:

In this discussion, students describe how a misunderstanding can lead to conflict and identify specific ways of effectively handling misunderstandings.

Character Traits:

Open-Mindedness, Fairness, Respect, Self-Control

Introducing the Topic:

In your own words, say to the students: *Today the topic is, "A Time I Was Involved in a Misunderstanding." Think of a time when you got into a conflict with someone based on a misunderstanding. Maybe you said something that was understood as a put down when you intended it as a joke. Perhaps you didn't call someone, or were accused of talking behind a friend's back, or said something to one person that was misquoted to another. Maybe you made a gesture or a face that was misunderstood and caused someone to react in anger. Or perhaps someone else did something like this and <u>you</u> were the one who misunderstood. Think about it for a few moments. Then tell us about an incident like this in your life, and how you handled it. The topic is, "A Time I Was Involved in a Misunderstanding."*

Discussion Questions:

— *When you realize that you have misunderstood someone, what can you do to help clear up the problem?*
— *What can you do when it appears that someone has misunderstood something you have said or done?*
— *What causes us to misunderstand the words and actions of others?*

Your Questions:

Something That Really Bothers Me

Purpose:

This topic invites students to describe things that typically annoy or upset them, and to discuss ways of handling irritations and annoyances.

Character Traits:

Self-Control, Self-Discipline

Introducing the Topic:

In your own words, say to the students: *Today our topic is, "Something That Really Bothers Me." Most of us can name one or more things that are guaranteed to annoy or upset us. What's one of yours? Maybe you're bothered by people who smoke—or people who criticize smokers. Perhaps you're bothered by loud television commercials, or dirty dishes in the sink, or the sound of chalk scraping across the chalkboard. Does dishonesty upset you? Are you annoyed by people who don't pay attention in class? Think it over, and tell us what bothers you—and how you handle your feelings. The topic is, "Something That Really Bothers Me."*

Discussion Questions:

— *What do the things we mentioned in our sharing session have to do with our values?*
— *Since the thing that bothers you isn't likely to go away, what can you do to control your feelings?*
— *Have you ever become involved in a conflict because of the thing that bothers you? How did it happen?*

Your Questions:

I Got Involved in a Conflict Because Something Unfair Was Happening to Someone Else

Purpose:

This topic encourages students to discuss some of the problems associated with taking a stand based on principle, and with becoming involved in the conflicts of others.

Character Traits:

Empathy, Fairness, Responsibility, Assertiveness, Courage

Introducing the Topic:

In your own words, say to the students: *Today's topic is, "I Got Involved in a Conflict Because Something Unfair Was Happening to Someone Else." This is something fairly common to us all. Maybe you saw a fight in progress between two people, and one of them was much stronger and bigger than the other. Perhaps someone had a particular viewpoint on something, and a few other people disagreed, so they ganged up and tried to punish the person for his or her opinion. Or maybe an adult was unfairly blaming a kid for something you knew wasn't the kid's responsibility. Whatever the exact situation, you became involved because you felt that something very unjust was going on. Can you think of such a time? Please don't say the names of the people involved or tell us their relationship to you. The topic is, "I Got Involved in a Conflict Because Something Unfair Was Happening to Someone Else."*

Discussion Questions:

— How can you determine when it's right to get involved in someone else's conflict and when it's not?
— Why do you think people sometimes become bullies?
— What have you learned about conflict from this session?
— What have you learned about standing up for something you believe is right?

Your Questions:

A Time I Controlled Myself and the Situation Well

Purpose:

This topic encourages students to describe a conflict or emergency situation in which they acted responsibly, and to discuss the importance of self-control in difficult situations.

Character Traits:

Self-Control, Self-Discipline, Positive Attitude, Confidence, Determination, Responsibility

Introducing the Topic:

In your own words, say to the students: *Today we have a challenging topic. It is, "A Time I Controlled Myself and the Situation Well." This session gives you a chance to take some deserved credit for handling a difficult circumstance with a cool head. Can you think of a time when you did that?*

Give it some thought. Perhaps you can remember a time when two or more people were upset with each other, or with you, but you kept the situation from getting out of hand. Or maybe you took charge in an emergency and helped people stay calm and orderly. Perhaps you acted instinctively, without really thinking it through, or perhaps you saw clearly what could happen if the situation wasn't controlled. In any case, you found the inner confidence to handle things in a way that you are now proud of. Tell us what happened and how you felt, but please don't mention any names. The topic is, "A Time I Controlled Myself and the Situation Well."

Discussion Questions:

— How do you feel now about what you did in that situation?
— How do you feel when you lose control of yourself or a situation?
— How can you handle a situation well if you are not in control of yourself?
— What did you learn from this session about handling difficult situations?

Your Questions:

How I Handled a Disagreement with a Friend

Purpose:
In this discussion, the students describe conflict situations involving peers and examine different strategies for resolving conflicts.

Character Traits:
Respect, Open-Mindedness, Fairness, Positive Attitude, Self-Control

Introducing the Topic:
In your own words, say to the students: *All of us at one time or another have probably disagreed with a friend and had negative feelings as a result. So today let's talk about those times. Our topic is, "How I Handled a Disagreement with a Friend."*

The disagreement you describe may have been a major thing that led to the end of the friendship, or it may have been resolved in such a way that your friendship became even stronger. You can describe a disagreement that occurred when you were a child, or one that occurred very recently. The disagreement may have built up over a long period, or it may have been a one-of-a-kind situation that cropped up very suddenly. Try to recreate in your mind what happened, and <u>without telling us the name of your friend</u>, describe the situation and what you did. The topic is, "How I Handled a Disagreement with a Friend."

Discussion Questions:
— What are the most common feelings that disagreements generate?
— How do you usually respond to disagreements?
— What determines whether a disagreement is handled well or poorly?
— What strategies did you learn from this session that will help you handle future disagreements in a positive way?

Your Questions:

We Made Room For One More

Purpose:

This topic asks the students to describe how they responded to someone's need to be included. In the process, they discuss the need of people to belong and be accepted.

Character Traits:

Empathy, Open-Mindedness, Fairness, Generosity

Introducing the Topic:

In your own words, say to the students: *Today, we're going to talk about inclusion and exclusion. Our topic is, "We Made Room for One More." Think of a time when you made an effort to include someone. Maybe you and your friends found enough room in the car for an extra person who wanted to go with you to a game or party. Or perhaps you knew someone who really wanted to be part of an organization or group you belong to, and you made an effort to get that person involved. How did you feel? Was this an easy thing for you to do, or did you have to pull some strings? If you had the chance to do it again, would you? Think about it for a few moments. The topic is, "We Made Room for One More."*

Discussion Questions:

— *How did the person who was included seem to feel?*
— *How do you feel about having the power to include someone?*
— *Why do we feel the need to belong to groups?*
— *How does it feel to be excluded?*
— *How can a person who is excluded most of the time learn the social skills that groups teach us?*

Your Questions:

I Wanted To Be Part of a Group, But Was Left Out

Purpose:

This topic asks students to describe a personal experience in which they were excluded or rejected. It also helps them to verbalize negative feelings associated with being left out, and to discuss ways of dealing with rejection.

Character Traits:

Empathy, Open-Mindedness, Fairness

Introducing the Topic:

In your own words, say to the students: *Today's topic is, "I Wanted to Be Part of a Group, But Was Left Out." Think of a time when you had your hopes set on being with a certain group of people—a club, an organization, or a bunch of friends—but it didn't happen. What happened in the situation? What caused your exclusion? Perhaps it was an event that had been planned very carefully, or maybe it was just a spur-of-the-moment activity. Did something unexpected come up, or did you kind of know you might be left out? Take a moment and trace in your mind the sequence of events leading up to your being excluded. What feelings did you have when you thought you were going to be with this group? What were your feelings later? The topic for today is, "I Wanted to Be Part of a Group, But Was Left Out."*

Note: Since this is a challenging topic, consider taking your turn first.

Discussion Questions:

— When you found out you weren't going to be included, how did you feel?
— What did you feel like doing, and what did you actually do?
— Was one of the common reactions to not being included a desire to find someone to blame? Does this help?
— What can you do when you notice that someone is being excluded from a group to which you belong?

Your Questions:

A Situation in Which I Behaved Responsibly

Purpose:

This topic challenges students to define responsible behavior, describe a situation in which they behaved responsibly, and discuss the benefits of responsible behavior.

Character Traits:

Responsibility, Self-Control, Self-Discipline, Positive Attitude

Introducing the Topic:

In your own words, say to the students: *Today in our circle session, we are going to take some deserved credit. The topic is, "A Situation in Which I Behaved Responsibly." Before we go any further, let's take a couple of minutes to talk about what responsible behavior is and why people think it's so great. Do you have any ideas?*

Listen to the students' comments. Then, in your own words, explain: *The word itself, response-able, says a lot. It means being __able__ to respond, to do something you think is right, not just sit there and do nothing. In other words, when you take care of a situation and yourself, you've behaved responsibly. You can feel proud of yourself. It may have been simple, or it may have been hard, but you did it!*

Think that over. You can probably remember lots of times when you behaved responsibly. See if there isn't one you'd like to tell us about. If there is, we'd like to hear what happened, how you felt, and what you did. The topic is, "A Situation in Which I Behaved Responsibly."

Discussion Questions:

— *How do you feel now about the responsible behavior you described?*
— *What rewards do you get for responsible behavior?*
— *What are some of the consequences of irresponsible behavior?*
— *Did you hear any good ideas for ways to behave responsibly that you might not have thought of before?*

Your Questions:

A Time I Talked to Someone I Was Afraid to Talk To

Purpose:

This topic asks students to describe how they overcame the fear of talking to an other person, to identify reasons people fear interacting with others, and to discuss methods of overcoming those fears.

Character Traits:

Positive Attitude, Perserverence, Self-Discipline, Courage

Introducing the Topic:

In your own words, say to the students: *Today we're going to talk about, "A Time I Talked to Someone I Was Afraid to Talk To." This is probably one of the most common fears among people — teenagers, little kids, and adults alike. At the same time, it's one of those fears that many people think they alone have! Think back. See if you can remember being almost too intimidated by someone to utter a word, yet somehow overcoming your fear and talking with the person. Perhaps the person was very important, or unpredictable, or in a position to hurt you in some way. Maybe you were afraid that the person wouldn't like you, or that you'd say something stupid. Tell us the circumstances and how you controlled your fear. If the incident involved anyone we know, please don't mention his or her name. The topic is, "A Time I Talked to Someone I Was Afraid to Talk To."*

Discussion Questions:

— *How did this person act toward you when you talked to him or her?*
— *What feelings did you have before and after you actually spoke to the person?*
— *What causes us to feel intimidated by some people?*
— *What can you say or do to bolster your courage in such situations?*

Your Questions:

Someone Handled a Problem Differently Than I'd Have Handled It

Purpose:

This topic encourages students to recognize differences in the way people handle problems and manage areas of their lives. In the process, they identify some of the benefits of keeping an open mind when confronted with differences in others.

Character Traits:

Open-Mindedness, Respect, Tolerance

Introducing the Topic:

In your own words, say to the students: *Today we're going to discuss the topic, "Someone Handled a Problem Differently Than I'd Have Handled It." Discovering new things about the people we know makes them interesting to us. We learn the different ways they think and how they react to certain situations. Sometimes the things we observe in others help us change and grow. Think of a time when you observed someone handling a problem very differently than you would have handled it. Maybe a friend was trying to fix something, and he or she went about it in a way that really surprised or puzzled you. Or perhaps a person you know had a problem involving strong emotions and controlled or expressed those feelings in a very unusual way — at least to your way of thinking. Think about it for a few moments. The topic is, "Someone Handled a Problem Differently Than I'd Have Handled it."*

Discussion Questions:

— Why do people respond to problems differently?
— The famous Italian film director, Frederico Fellini, once said, "Accept me as I am; only then will we discover each other." What do you think he meant?
— What happens to us if we close our minds to ideas and ways of behaving that are different from our own?
— Why is it important in life to be open-minded?

Your Questions:

An Experience That Caused Me to See Things Differently

Purpose:

This topic invites the students to describe an experience that significantly changed their perception. In the process, they examine how perceptions are colored by experience and vice versa.

Character Trait:

Open-Mindedness

Introducing the Topic:

In your own words, say to the students: *Today our topic is, "An Experience That Caused Me to See Things Differently." Have you ever thought about how your perceptions affect your experiences and vice versa? Lots of times we interpret events based on beliefs and viewpoints that we already have. Occasionally, an experience can cause us to shift our point of view and see things in a different way. For example, perhaps someone you didn't like very well unexpectedly did you a favor, and suddenly you saw the person in a new light. Or maybe an important world event profoundly affected the lives of many people and caused you to view your own life differently. Maybe the experience that changed your perception occurred while you were watching a movie, reading a book, working on a project, or trying to solve a tough problem. If you would like to share with the group, tell us about, "An Experience That Caused Me to See Things Differently."*

Discussion Questions:

— *Did you notice any similarities in the kinds of experiences that caused us to see things differently?*
— *How are our perceptions and belief systems formed in the first place?*
— *Why is it difficult for some people to change their perceptions even in the face of overwhelming evidence that says those perceptions are wrong?*

Your Questions:

How I Learned to Get Along With Someone Who Doesn't Think the Way I Do

Purpose:

In this discussion, students describe how they get along with a person whose values and beliefs are different from their own. In the process they verbalize some of the benefits of interacting with people of diverse values/beliefs.

Character Traits:

Open-Mindedness, Empathy, Respect

Introducing the Topic:

In your own words, say to the students: *The topic of this session is, "How I Learned to Get Along With Someone Who Doesn't Think the Way I Do." We've all had experiences where we've had to get along with people who don't think the way we do. This can happen with neighbors, friends, classmates, and family members.*

Think of one person you learned to get along with who didn't think the way you did. How did you overcome this barrier? Did you hide your own feelings and thoughts? Did you try to get your way by using tricks or games? Or did you accept the person and feel acceptance from him or her? If you decide to share, tell us what you did and why you think your approach worked, without telling us the name of the person. Our topic is, "How I Learned to Get Along with Someone Who Doesn't Think the Way I Do."

Discussion Questions:

— *What did you hear in this session that might be useful to you in learning to get along with others?*
— *What would life be like if all people were the same?*
— *How do we benefit from accepting, and even encouraging, diverse points of view?*

Your Questions:

Two Things I Believe In That Conflict With Each Other

Purpose:

This topic asks students to identify values they hold that sometimes conflict, and to identify methods for resolving such conflicts.

Character Traits:

Responsibility, Self-Management

Introducing the Topic:

In your own words, say to the students: *Our topic today is, "Two Things I Believe In That Conflict With Each Other." Very often, we create dilemmas for ourselves by trying to live up to values and beliefs that don't always fit together well. For example, I believe in saving gasoline. I also believe in being on time for appointments. Now, you wouldn't think that those two values could conflict with each other, but they can and sometimes do. Here's how it works: When I'm late for an appointment, I exceed the speed limit and waste gas.*

There are many areas where values can conflict. Loyalty is a good example. At what point does our loyalty to a friend become more or less important than our loyalty to rules or human rights? Has a friend ever asked you to do something that you know is wrong? When that happens, you have to decide which is more important, being with your friend or doing what you think is right. You've no doubt experienced many similar conflicts. Think of one that you'd be willing to share with us. Our topic is, "Two Things I Believe In That Conflict With Each Other."

Discussion Questions:

— How did you handle the conflict you shared?
— When you are in conflict, how do you feel? How do you act?
— What decision-making skills can we use to help resolve values conflicts?
— How is knowing what you value—what is most important to you—helpful when you are faced with conflicts like this?

Your Questions:

A Time When I Trusted Myself

Purpose:

To encourage students to acknowledge themselves for trusting their own instincts and abilities in specific situations. In the process, the students define trust, discuss the importance of, and ways of increasing, self-trust.

Character Traits:

Trustworthiness, Perseverance, Self-Control, Self-Discipline, Positive Attitude

Introducing the Topic:

In your own words, say to the students: *Our discussion topic today is, "A Time When I Trusted Myself." There are many times in our lives when we need to ask someone for help or advice. There are other times when we have to trust our own judgment and experience to solve problems for which only we have the solutions. Take a minute to think about a time when you trusted your own skills, knowledge, or experience. Maybe you trusted yourself to solve a personal problem, or to make the right choice between two or more equally attractive (or unattractive) alternatives. You might have trusted yourself to come through as you walked to the podium to deliver a speech, approached the plate to defend your team's title, or stepped up to the microphone to sing or play a solo. Think about it for a moment. The topic is, "A Time When I Trusted Myself."*

Discussion Questions:

— *What feelings did you have when you realized that you trusted yourself enough to handle the situation?*
— *What is trust?*
— *What methods can you use to learn to trust yourself more?*
— *What are some circumstances under which you should always seek help from someone else?*

Your Questions:

I Made a Decision Based on My Values

Purpose:
To help students become conscious of the role of their values in guiding their everyday decisions.

Character Traits:
Ethical Decision Making, and all positive values identified during the session

Introducing the Topic:
In your own words, say to the students: *The topic today is, "I Made a Decision Based on My Values." Making this kind of decision is not an unusual event. We all make many choices daily because of things that are important to us or things we strongly believe in. Think of one example from your own experience and describe it to us. Maybe you decided to assist a classmate who was having trouble with a math problem — not because you had to, but because you believe that it is important to help others. Perhaps you decided to tell the truth about something, even though telling the truth caused someone to get angry at you. You did it because you value honesty. Or maybe you decided to clean up your trash after lunch because you want to show respect for the environment. Have you ever decided to keep a secret no matter what? Did you do it because you value being a trustworthy person? Have you ever reported a crime? Do you listen when someone else is speaking? Do you do these things because you know they are the responsible, respectful things to do? We all make many decisions every day. Tell us about one that was guided by a value. Our topic is, "I Made a Decision Based on My Values."*

Discussion Questions:
— How did you feel when you made the decision you described?
— Why is it important to be guided by values?
— How can you be sure that your values are the right ones?
— Where do we learn our values?

Your Questions:

An Agreement That Was Hard to Keep

Purpose:

This topic asks students to describe commitments that were difficult to honor. During the discussion, they verbalize the importance of keeping agreements and discuss what can be done when an agreement is too difficult to keep.

Character Traits:

Responsibility, Self-Control, Self-Discipline, Trustworthiness, Perseverance

Introducing the Topic:

In your own words, say to the students: *Today our topic is, "An Agreement That Was Hard to Keep." Think of a time when it was very hard for you to keep an agreement or commitment. For example, maybe you agreed to do something for a family member or friend that turned out to be very difficult. Or perhaps you made a commitment to finish a project at school in less time than you really needed.*

You can go either way in responding to this topic. You can talk about a time you kept your commitment, even though it was difficult, or you can describe a situation in which you were unable or unwilling to follow through. Maybe your agreement didn't seem so overwhelming at first, but after you got into it, you found out that it involved a great deal of time or energy. On the other hand, perhaps you knew right from the beginning what you were getting into. Tell us what happened, and how you handled it. The topic is, "An Agreement That Was Hard to Keep."

Discussion Questions:

— *How did you feel about the agreement when you realized it would be hard to keep?*
— *What can you do when you realize you won't be able to keep a commitment?*
— *Should you always avoid making agreements that might be hard to keep? Why or why not?*
— *What did you learn from this session about responsible behavior?*

Your Questions:

I Didn't Do Something Because I Knew It Would Hurt Someone

Purpose:
This topic asks students to describe a time when they modified their behavior out of concern for another person. As part of the discussion, they describe positive feelings derived from showing concern for others.

Character Traits:
Responsibility, Self-Control, Self-Discipline, Empathy

Introducing the Topic:
In your own words, say to the students: *One of the most important concepts that relates to responsibility has to do with recognizing your own power to affect other people, and using that power in a respectful way. The topic for this session is, "I Didn't Do Something Because I Knew It Would Hurt Someone."*

Can you think of a time when you knew someone would get hurt if you did something, so you didn't do it? Perhaps it was easy for you to decide not to do this thing, or maybe it was a tough decision because part of you really wanted to do it. Maybe you stopped other people from doing it, too. Perhaps you wouldn't go along with some friends because you realized that somebody would end up getting hurt. Without mentioning names, tell us what you didn't do and how you felt about your decision. The topic is, "I Didn't Do Something Because I Knew It Would Hurt Someone."

Discussion Questions:
— How do you feel about yourself when you are considerate of other people?
— How do you feel when someone demonstrates that he or she cares what happens to you?
— When is it right to do something, even though you know it will probably hurt another person?

Your Questions:

Something Nice I Did for a Friend

Purpose:

This topic focuses attention on the kinds of behaviors that are positive, helpful and appreciated by others, and thereby increases student awareness of effective modes of social interaction.

Character Traits:

Empathy, Caring, Self-Discipline, Sociability, Positive Attitude, Compassion

Introducing the Topic:

In your own words, say to the students: *Today, we're going to talk about "Something Nice I Did for a Friend." Think about all the times when you've done nice things for your friends and choose one incident to share. Maybe you surprised your friend with a present, a party, or a special outing on his or her birthday. Perhaps your friend asked you for a favor and you granted that favor gladly because you knew that your help would be appreciated. It doesn't matter whether the nice thing you did was small and simple or big and difficult. The important thing is it was a nice thing to do. The topic is, "Something Nice I Did for a Friend."*

Discussion Questions:

— *How did you feel when you did a nice thing for your friend?*
— *How did your friend seem to feel? How could you tell he or she felt that way?*
— *Why is it important to do nice things for our friends?*
— *Why is it important to let people know when they do something that's nice?*

Your Questions:

Someone Did Something for Me That I Appreciated

Purpose:

This topic encourages students to recall times when others have given them assistance and how they responded to these acts of kindness.

Character Traits:

Caring, Sociability, Positive Attitude

Introducing the Topic:

In your own words, say to the students: *Today's circle session topic is, "Someone Did Something for Me That I Appreciated." Have you ever had someone do something for you that you thought was out of the ordinary, or unexpected, or particularly nice? Tell us about it.*

The person could have been a member of your family, a teacher, or a friend. Maybe a brother or sister offered to help you with a difficult task, or a friend brought you a book to read when you were home with the flu. Perhaps you received an unexpected birthday greeting, or a phone call from someone who wanted to wish you good luck in a big game. Think for a moment about something like this that's happened to you. If you let the person know how you felt, tell us about that, too. The topic for today is, "Someone Did Something for Me That I Appreciated."

Discussion Questions:

— *Did you notice any similarities in the things we shared?*
— *What are some other ways that people influence each other's feelings?*
— *How did you feel about the person when they did the thing you appreciated? How do you think the person felt about him/herself for doing something for someone else?*
— *What value do you see in doing nice things for other people?*

Your Questions:

Something I Taught Myself

Purpose:

This topic helps students to realize that learning is something they frequently accomplish on their own, and that they have ultimate control over what, how much, and how quickly they learn.

Character Traits:

Perseverance, Determination, Self-Discipline, Positive Attitude, Self-Management, Self-Control

Introducing the Topic:

In your own words, say to the students: *Today we are going to discuss the topic, "Something I Taught Myself." You are invited to share anything, large or small, that you learned to do on your own. Maybe you taught yourself basic computer skills, or read your first book without any help from parents or teachers. Perhaps you figured out how to solve a particular type of math problem, or learned a new sport. Did you teach yourself how to ride a bike, skate, draw, do a magic trick, or cook spaghetti? Describe what you learned, how you taught it to yourself, and how you felt when you realized that you had learned it. The topic is, "Something I Taught Myself."*

Discussion Questions:

— *What feelings did most of us have after we successfully taught ourselves something?*

— *Knowing that you have taught yourself certain skills, how do you feel about your ability to learn other things?*

— *How much of the responsibility for learning is up to you? How much is up to your teachers or parents?*

Your Questions:

What Good Friends Need From Each Other

Purpose:

This topic asks students to think about their own friendships and identify personal qualities and ways of interacting that strengthen them. Students develop a generalized understanding of the ingredients of healthy relationships.

Character Traits:

Empathy, Respect, Caring, Trustworthiness, Sociability, Positive Attitude, Self-Control

Introducing the Topic:

In your own words, say to the students: *The topic for today's session is, "What Good Friends Need From Each Other." There are many things that go into making a good friendship. You might want to think about some of your good friendships and what you give to, and get from, those relationships that makes them work. How important are things like shared interests, understanding, time spent together, and gift-giving? Tell us about one or two things you think people need in order to be friends. Our topic is, "What Good Friends Need From Each Other."*

Discussion Questions:

— What ingredients did most of us think were needed in a good friendship?
— How do you feel when you don't get what you want in a friendship?
— How do you feel when your friend gives you all the things you need?
— What makes friendships last a long time?

Your Questions:

I Had a Hard Time Choosing Between Two Things

Purpose:

This topic encourages students to identify choices they have made and explain that choosing one thing often means giving up others.

Character Traits:

Ethical Decsion-Making, Integrity, Self Discipline

Introducing the Topic:

In your own words, say to the students: *Our topic for this session has to do with decision making, and I'm sure all of us will be able to relate to it. Have you ever been in a situation where you were torn between two things and couldn't make up your mind? If so, you'll appreciate this topic. It is, "I Had a Hard Time Choosing Between Two Things."*

Tell us about a time when you had to choose one thing over another because we couldn't have both. Maybe you wanted to go to two different places at the same time, or you wanted to buy two things and only had enough money for one. Maybe you wanted to do or have one thing, but you knew that the "right" thing to do was choose something else. Describe some other type of situation in which you had to choose between two different things. Think about it for a few moments. The topic is, "I Had a Hard Time Choosing Between Two Things."

Discussion Questions:

— How did you feel about giving up the thing you didn't choose?
— How is making a decision the same thing as taking a risk?
— Is the best choice for one person the best choice for everyone? Why?
— How do your values help you to make a decision?

Your Questions:

How I Showed Someone That I Could Be Trusted

Purpose:
By focusing on trust-building in a specific relationship, the students identify trust as an important component of all good relationships and recognize how their behavior contributes to, or undermines, that trust.

Character Traits:
Trustworthiness, Responsibility, Respect, Self-Discipline, Ethical Decision Making, Sociability, Self-Management

Introducing the Topic:
In your own words, say to the students: *Today's topic is, "How I Showed Someone That I Could Be Trusted." Think about a time when you wanted someone to trust you. Maybe it was a parent or other relative, or it could have been a friend, teacher, or coach. Perhaps you were hoping that this person would give you a privilege you'd never had before, or trust you to take care of something that belonged to them. Anytime we take on additional responsibilities, we are asking people to trust us. Describe the circumstances of your situation, and tell us how you convinced the other person that you could be trusted. Did you simply talk the person into trusting you? Or did you have to demonstrate your reliability? Think about it for a few moments. The topic is, "How I Showed Someone That I Could Be Trusted."*

Discussion Questions:
— Why was trust important to the relationship you described?
— How can letting someone know that you trust them, encourage them to trust you?
— Once you've earned someone's trust, how long does that trust last?

Your Questions:

A Time When I Misunderstood What Someone Said

Purpose:

This topic asks students to trace the development of a misunderstanding caused by poor communication. In the process of sharing, they examine the components of good communication, particularly listening.

Character Traits:

Positive Attitude, Responsibility, Respect, Caring, Self-Discipline

Introducing the Topic:

In your own words, say to the students: *Misunderstandings between people are inevitable. They are often communication problems, like the type we are going to talk about today. Our topic is, "A Time When I Misunderstood What Someone Said."*

Without mentioning any names, tell us about a time when someone said something to you, but the message got twisted and you understood something quite different from what was actually said. For example, maybe you thought a friend said something negative to you, and were upset for hours. Or perhaps you misunderstood the directions for a homework assignment and turned it in all wrong. Tell us what caused the misunderstanding and how it got cleared up, if at all. By talking about misunderstandings maybe we'll learn a bit about good communication and avoiding misunderstandings in the future. Once again, our topic is, "A Time When I Misunderstood What Someone Said."

Discussion Questions:

— How did you feel when you realized you had understood the other person?
— How did the other person seem to feel?
— In the future when you realize that you have misunderstood someone, what is one thing that you could do to help clear up the problem?
— What can you do when it appears that someone else has misunderstood what you have said?
— How does good listening help prevent misunderstandings?

Your Questions:

How I Would Like To Be Known by Others

Purpose:

This topic gives the students an opportunity to identify character traits that they value and would like to possess in the eyes of others. The first step to developing positive character traits is to identify and describe them.

Character Traits:

Empathy, Caring, Sociability, Positive Attitude, Self-Management

Introducing the Topic:

In your own words, say to the students: *Today's topic is, "How I Would Like To Be Known by Others." Have you ever thought about the impression that people form of you? What are your ideas about how you would like others to see you, or how you would like others to feel about you? Maybe you want others to know you as a caring, or honest, or hard-working person. Maybe you want to be know as a good athlete or good student. The things that you want to be known as are really the things that you value. So think about it and tell us about the kinds of things you would like for other people to think about you. The topic is, "How I Would Like To Be Known by Others."*

Discussion Questions:

— What characteristics and qualities did we mention most?
— How do you think you would feel if you knew that others saw you as (an honest) person?
— What are the things you need to do to show others that you are (an honest) person?
— How do you feel about other people who possess the qualities that you want to possess?

Your Questions:

I Reached Out To Someone Who Needed A Friend

Purpose:

Students describe a time when they were sensitive to the needs of another person and chose to help meet those needs by giving of themselves. They students recognize their power to positively affect the feelings of others.

Character Traits:

Self-Control, Determination, Responsibility, Positive Attitude

Introducing the Topic:

In your own words, say to the students: *Today we're going to talk about behaving in a friendly manner. The topic is, "I Reached Out To Someone Who Needed A Friend." Think about a time when you knew that someone needed a friend very much, so you did or said something to show the person that you wanted to be friends. Maybe you helped a new kid in school get acquainted with other kids. Or perhaps you comforted a classmate whose parent had recently died. Whatever the specific situation, you recognized that the other person was feeling lonely, or scared, or dejected, and offered you support. Without using any names, tell us how the other person was feeling and what you did to reach out in friendship. The topic is, "I Reached Out To Someone Who Needed A Friend."*

Discussion Questions;

— *How did you feel about yourself when you reached out in a friendly way?*
— *Do you always have to wait until you notice someone is feeling badly to reach out?*
— *How did the person react to you when you reached out to him or her?*
— *How does it make you feel when you are "down and out," and somebody is friendly toward you?*

Your Questions:

A Time I Was Really Angry, But I Was Able To Calm Myself Down

Purpose:

to focus on the benefits of positive responses to anger and to allow students to exchange information about methods for calming themselves down after becoming extreme stressed by anger.

Character Traits:

Courage (and other positive character traits mentioned during the discussion)

Introducing the Topic:

In your own words say to the students: *We all experience times when something happens and we feel very angry. Anger is a difficult emotion to handle. Being able to release this feeling and move on is hard, but it can be done. Our topic is, "A Time I Was Really Angry, But I Was Able To Calm Myself Down."*

Think about a time when you were very angry, but helped yourself get over those feelings by doing something that calmed you down. Maybe you just walked away, or counted to ten, or perhaps you took several deep breaths. Did you work your anger out by doing something physical like running or dancing? Without mentioning names, tell us what made you angry, how you calmed yourself down, and how well your calming method worked. Our topic is, "A Time I Was Really Angry, But I Was Able To Calm Myself Down."

Discussion Questions:

— What calming methods seemed to work best for most of us?
— What ideas did you get about ways to help yourself calm down in the future?
— Why is it important to learn methods for controlling anger? What would happen if people experienced their anger in violent ways?

Your Questions:

Someone Who Demonstrated a Lot of Courage

Purpose:

This topic asks students to identify specific acts of courage, to focus on the value of courageous behavior, and to identify other character traits associated with valor.

Character Traits:

Responsibility, Self-Discipline, Self-Management, Ethical Decision Making

Introducing the Topic:

In your own words say to the students: *Today's topic is, "Someone Who Demonstrated a Lot of Courage." People show courage in many ways. We all know about people who have done something that demonstrated courage. Some people are courageous in the way they handle an illness or serious injury. A fire fighter who goes off to fight a terrible fire and rescues someone from the burning building is usually seen as courageous. People who spoke out or demonstrated on behalf of civil rights in the U.S. and South Africa, knowing that they might be hurt or jailed for their actions, were courageous. Tell us about someone that you know personally, or have heard about, such as a famous historical figure, who demonstrated courage. Our topic is, "Someone Who Demonstrated a Lot of Courage."*

Discussion Questions:

— What other character traits were demonstrated by the courageous people we described?
— What enables people to demonstrate courage?
— What makes it hard sometimes for people to be courageous?
— Why do courageous people often become role models?
— How do we feel about people who show courage?
— What have you learned from this discussion about how you can show courage?

Your Questions:

A Good Choice That I'm Glad I Made

Purpose:

This topic encourages students to acknowledge themselves for making positive choices. It also focuses on the decision-making process and on the benefits of choosing well.

Character Traits:

Generosity, Empathy, Responsibility, Caring, Trustworthiness, Self-Discipline, Sociability, Positive Attitude, Self-Management

Introducing the Topic:

In your own words say to the students: *Our topic for today is, "A Good Choice That I'm Glad I Made." Making a choice means picking one action over others, like choosing to read a book instead of watch TV or play outdoors, or choosing to eat an apple instead of a cookie. A choice can also involve things you say. For example, you can choose to say, "Please excuse me," instead of, "Get out of my way." Can you think of a choice that you made recently and you feel good about now? Maybe you chose to clean up your room, and you are glad because it looks nice now. Or perhaps you chose to study thoroughly and do all of your homework carefully, and now you are pleased because you feel confident and earned a good grade on a test. We all make many choices every day. Tell us about one that you made, and why you are glad you made it. The topic is, "A Good Choice That I'm Glad I Made."*

Discussion Questions:

— When you have several possible actions to choose from, how do you make a decision?
— How do you know that you have made the right decision?
— Why is it sometimes hard to choose the best or "right" things to do?
— How do you feel about yourself when you make the best choice?

Your Questions:

I Did Something That Made Me Feel Like a Good Person

Purpose:

Students recognize themselves and their classmates for specific good deeds. Social reinforcement for good behavior allows students to conclude that such behavior is even more meaningful and worthwhile than previously thought.

Character Traits:

Trustworthiness, Open-Mindedness, Tolerance, Respect, Courage

Introducing the Topic:

In your own words, say to the students: *Today our topic is "I Did Something That Made Me Feel Like a Good Person." Think about something you did that was worthwhile and made you feel good about yourself. It could have been something you did for an individual, like helping an elderly neighbor carry in groceries, or quickly turning down your music when you realized that it was bothering a visitor. Perhaps you cheerfully helped your family do yard work or visited a sick relative or friend. The thing that made you feel like a good person could have been something that no one else knew about, like picking up trash in the park. Think about it for a moment. When you are ready, the topic is, "I Did Something That Made Me Feel Like a Good Person."*

Discussion Questions:

— What was it about the thing you did that created feelings of satisfaction or pride?
— How do we learn to feel good about some actions and bad about others?
— What are some of the qualities of a good person?

Your Questions:

A Time Someone Was Being Treated Unfairly

Purpose:

This discussion enables students to describe negative feelings generated by unfair treatment, and to identify productive ways of handling those feelings.

Character Traits:

Fairness, Tolerance, Empathy, Respect, Caring, Sociability, Integrity

Introducing the Topic:

In your own words say to the students: *Today our topic is, "A Time Someone Was Being Treated Unfairly." Think of a situation in which someone was not being treated fairly. The person in the situation could have been you, or someone else. For example, maybe a kid was punished for something he or she didn't do. Or perhaps a person was ridiculed or teased for being overweight, or awkward, or speaking English poorly. The unfair treatment could have come from one person, or a group of people. Maybe it happened once, or repeatedly over a long period of time. Think of an example of unfair treatment that you know about, describe the situation and tell us how you felt. If you know how other people felt, tell us that too, but please don't mention any names. The topic is, "A Time Someone Was Being Treated Unfairly."*

Discussion Questions:

— *How did most of us seem to feel about the incident of unfair treatment we described?*
— *When we feel angry in response to unfair acts, how can we show our anger?*
— *What actions can we take when we're aware that people are being treated unfairly?*

Your Questions:

A Time When I Accepted Someone Else's Feelings

Purpose:

This topic invites students to share incidents in which they focused on and responded to the feelings of another person, even when those feelings were negative.

Character Traits:

Empathy, Open-Mindedness, Fairness, Ethical Decision Making, Self-Management, Tolerance

Introducing the Topic:

In your own words, say to the students: *As we all know, it means a lot to have our feelings accepted. When someone accepts your feelings, it almost like accepting you. In this session we are going to turn this idea around and talk about how it feels to be the acceptance giver. The topic is, "A Time When I Accepted Someone Else's Feelings."*

Can you remember a time when you gave your attention to someone and accepted his or her feelings? Maybe you listened carefully to a friend who was angry with you for breaking a promise. Or you may have accepted your parent's frustration about the condition of your room. Perhaps you listened to a teammate who accused you of playing unfairly or uncooperatively. Keep in mind that the most difficult feelings to accept are those that are different from your own, yet true acceptance means listening without getting angry, defensive, or judgmental. Think about it for a few moments. The topic is, "A Time When I Accepted Someone Else's Feelings."

Discussion Questions:

— When is it hardest to accept someone else's feelings?
— How can you discipline yourself to listen and accept negative feelings when they are directed at you?
— What is gained by accepting the feelings of others?

Your Questions:

How I Deal with Intolerance and Prejudice

Purpose:

This topic asks students to describe their reactions to acts of intolerance and prejudice and to evaluate the effectiveness of different kinds of responses.

Character Traits:

Tolerance, Open-Mindedness, Empathy, Respect, Fairness, Courage, Ethical Decision-Making, Self-Management

Introducing the Topic:

In your own words, say to the students, *Our topic today is, "How I Deal with Intolerance and Prejudice." Perhaps you can think of several different ways in which you have reacted to these things. If so, just tell us about the way you respond most often. You can describe your reaction to intolerance and prejudice directed at you, or directed at someone else in your presence. Or you might decide to tell us about intolerance and prejudice that you've discovered within yourself, and how you deal with that.*

Do you get angry and challenge the other person? Do you show your disapproval with an icy stare and a cold manner? Are you assertive in expressing your opposing views? Or do you tend to ignore the person and act as if nothing happened? If you like, tell us about a specific time you responded this way, and describe how you felt. Our topic is, "How I Deal with Intolerance and Prejudice."

Discussion Questions:

— How well does your method of dealing with prejudice and intolerance work?
— What happens as a result of your method? Are you satisfied with the results?
— What would happen if all the people who usually ignore intolerance started opposing it assertively?
— How do attitudes of tolerance lead to a better school/community/world?

Your Questions:

What I Think the World Needs To Be a Better Place

Purpose:

This topic asks students to envision a better world and identify things that could be done to achieve the improvement they imagine.

Character Traits:

Citizenship, Ethical Decision Making, Open-Mindedness

Introducing the Topic:

In your own words, say to the students: *The topic for today is, "What I Think the World Needs To Be a Better Place." How do you think the world could be improved? Would it be better if everyone had enough food to eat and had medical care? If people and countries talked to each other, would the world be improved? Would it be better if we all adopted the same environmental standards so that the world's air and water would be freer of pollution? Would you add more laughter and love and take away anger and hatred? Would you improve education and decrease weaponry? Think for a bit about all the things that could be done and describe the one you think most important. Today's topic is, "What I Think the World Needs To Be a Better Place."*

Discussion Questions:

— *What would it take to actually realize the improvements we talked about?*
— *What can you do to make the world a better place?*
— *How do your values affect how you responded to this topic?*

Your Questions:

Something I've Done (or Could Do) to Improve Our World

Purpose:

This topic engages students in describing ways in which they can contribute to the betterment of the community/world.

Character Traits:

Citizenship, Ethical Decision-Making, Integrity

Introducing the Topic:

In your own words, say to the students: *The topic for this session is, "Something I've Done (or Could Do) to Improve Our World." Can you think of a time when you did something that you felt really helped, even in a small way, to improve the world we live in? Perhaps you improved a condition of some kind on your street or in your community. Maybe you helped change something that you thought was wrong. Or perhaps you did something to help the ecology—like making careful use of resources like water and electricity, or treating animals with care. Whatever it is, we would like to hear about it. If you can't think of something you've already done, perhaps you can think of something you would like to do in the future, either independently or with a group. Our topic is, "Something I've Done (or Could Do) to Improve Our World."*

Discussion Questions:

— How are feelings of apathy developed?
— How are feelings of empathy developed?
— How can we create an atmosphere in this community/country that will encourage people to take action to improve things?
— How do you feel when you do something that helps improve our world?
— How do your values help determine what you view as important and contributing to a better world?

Your Questions:

One of My Favorite Possessions

Purpose:

This topic invites the students to describe an possession that has special meaning for them. In the process they examine the values they hold that make the item special.

Character Traits:

Caring, Positive Attitude, Ethical Decision Making, Respect

Introducing the Topic:

In your own words, say to the students: *Our topic for today is, "One of My Favorite Possessions." You probably own several things that are special to you. You may have had some of these possessions since you were very young, and you probably acquired others more recently. Tell us about one special thing you own, and describe what makes that item special. Someone you care for very much may have given it to you, or you may have done extra chores to earn enough money to buy it. It could be something that's fun to wear, or play with, or that looks nice in your room. Think about it for a moment. The topic is, "One of My Favorite Possessions."*

Discussion Questions:

— *What is it that makes certain things special to us?*
— *Do you think it's important for people to have favorite possessions? Why or why not?*
— *How do your values help you decide which of your possessions are favorites?*

Your Questions:

How I Feel About War

Purpose:

This topic asks the students to express their feelings about a difficult and complex topic — war. In the process, they are encouraged to examine the values upon which those feelings are based.

Character Traits:

Generosity, Self-Discipline, Positive Attitude, Empathy, Caring, Compassion, Ethical Decision Making

Introducing the Topic:

In your own words, say to the students: *Today's topic is, "How I Feel About War." Feelings are facts. Feelings are not right or wrong, they just are. Your feelings are uniquely your own and, at the same time, they may be similar to the feelings of others. Sometimes your feelings are mixed. You feel good and bad about the same thing. Today we're going to describe our feelings about war. We have not experienced a war in this country for a long time. However, we have participated in armed conflicts in other parts of the world. Examples of such conflicts are World War II, the Korean War, Vietnam and the Gulf War. How do you feel about war? Do you feel good, bad, glad, sad, scared, or angry? Perhaps you have more than one feeling when you think about war. Take a few moments to get in touch with your feelings. The topic is, "How I Feel About War."*

Discussion Questions:

— *What similarities did you notice in the feelings that were shared?*
— *How do you suppose you developed your feelings about war?*
— *What values that you hold help to determine how your feel?*
— *What can you do to influence your country's actions with respect to peace and war?*

Topic Variations

"How I Feel About the Homeless"
"How I Feel About the Environment"
"How I Feel About Discrimination"
"How I Feel About Drugs"
"How I Feel About World Hunger"

This is a very powerful forum for any number of variations. You may tie into a particular classroom learning theme, an event that involves your students, or some unsettling news in the media. It is very important not to judge feelings as they are shared. The purpose of this circle is to get students in touch with their feelings and to examine their values.

It Made Me Feel Good to Make Someone Else Feel Good

Purpose:

This topic is designed to highlight the personal benefits of consciously choosing to do things for others.

Character Trait:

Ethical Decision Making

Introducing the Topic:

In your own words, say to the students: *The topic today is, "It Made Me Feel Good to Make Someone Else Feel Good." When we contribute to good feelings in others, we usually feel good ourselves. In fact, we sometimes benefit as much as the recipient. Think of a time when you enjoyed positive feelings by making someone else feel good.*

Maybe you helped a new student find a classroom, or went out of your way to compliment someone's appearance. Perhaps you helped someone understand a difficult math concept, or taught a new player how to pitch a curve ball. You may have stood up for someone who was being bullied or teased. Or you may have helped an elderly neighbor carry groceries. Tell us about one time when you helped another person feel good and in the process felt good yourself. The topic is, "It Made Me Feel Good to Make Someone Else Feel Good."

Discussion Questions:

— Why do we feel good when we help someone else feel good?
— What sort of planning is required to make someone feel good?
— What would this school be like if we all spent a little more time helping others feel good?

Your Questions:

I Had a Problem and Solved It

Purpose:

This topic invites the students to examine problem-solving approaches they have successfully used in the past, and enables them to identify specific strategies that they can call upon to solve future problems.

Character Traits:

Perseverance, Self-Control, Self-Discipline, Determination, Responsibility

Introducing the Topic:

In your own words, say to the students: *Today's session focuses on something you did in the past, so take a moment to think back. The topic is, "I Had A Problem and Solved It." Problems are something we all have throughout life. It's not possible to live without problems, but it is possible to solve them.*

Think of a problem that you experienced some time in your past and solved. Maybe it had to do with a class or requirement at school. Perhaps the problem was associated with a close friendship, or was centered around your home life. If you choose to share, describe the problem, how you solved it, and the feelings you had when you managed it successfully. Our topic is, "I Had a Problem and Solved It."

Discussion Questions:

— *What did you learn from this session about problems?*
— *What are some problem-solving strategies that you heard mentioned today?*
— *How can you use these strategies when faced with future problems?*

Your Questions:

Things I Do To Keep a Friend

Purpose:

This topic helps the students to increase their understanding of how friendships form and develop. It also highlights the need in friendships for such values as respect and trust.

Character Traits:

Respect, Trustworthiness, Positive Attitude, Tolerance, Caring, Self-Discipline, Sociability

Introducing the Topic:

In your own words, say to the students: *Our topic for today is, "Things I Do to Keep a Friend." A friend is someone about whom we have special feelings. For all of us, having friends is important. So is keeping them. We all have special ways of expressing our friendship, such as making time for a friend, talking with and listening to a friend, and giving thoughtful gifts or cards. What do you do to keep a friend? Maybe you simply tell your friend how much you value his or her friendship. You may go places or do things that your friend enjoys, even when you'd rather be doing something else. Close your eyes for a moment and think of the many things you do to keep a friend. Our topic is, "The Things I Do to Keep a Friend."*

Discussion Questions:

— *Why is it important to work at keeping friendships alive?*
— *How do your friends feel about the things you do?*
— *What would happen if you didn't do anything to keep your friendships going?*
— *How important is respect in a friendship? ...Trust? ...Responsibility? ...Forgiveness?*

Your Questions:

People Seem to Respect Me When...

Purpose:

This topic asks students to identify personal qualities or behaviors that earn the respect of other people. In the process, the students recognize the influence that respect has on self-esteem.

Character Traits:

Respect, Sociability, Positive Attitude

Introducing the Topic:

In your own words, say to the students: *Our topic for this session is, "People Seem to Respect Me When...." To respect a person is to admire and hold that person in high regard or esteem. When do people seem to respect you? Is it when you tell the truth or follow through on what you say you will do? Perhaps people seem to respect you when you get good grades or demonstrate the ability to solve problems. Perhaps you notice the respect of others when you employ a good strategy to win a game, or come home on time, or complete your homework regularly. Standing by your convictions, even though they are unpopular, and your ability to say no when appropriate will always inspire respect. Take a few moments to think of something you do that people respect. Our topic is, "People Seem to Respect Me When...."*

Discussion Questions:

— *Why is it important to earn the respect of others?*
— *How can you tell whether someone respects you?*
— *What are some things that can lead to a loss of respect on the part of others?*

Your Questions:

Somebody Whose Opinion I Value Very Much

Purpose:

This topic encourages the students to identify opinions they value and to recognize the influence that the individuals who hold those opinions have on them.

Character Traits:

Respect, Caring, Ethical Decision Making

Introducing the Topic:

In your own words, say to the students: Our topic for this session is, *"Somebody Whose Opinion I Value Very Much." This topic gives us a chance to talk about someone we admire and whose opinions we respect. This could be someone you know personally, such as an older brother or sister, a friend, or a neighbor whom you look up to and are able to talk with. Or it could be someone you don't know personally but whose opinions you respect, like a TV personality, a movie star, or a politician. Think about it for a minute and, if you will, tell us a little about one person who's opinion you value. The topic is, "Somebody Whose Opinion I Value Very Much."*

Discussion Questions:

— *Did you notice any similar characteristics in the people whose opinions we value?*
— *What character traits does this person have that you like?*
— *How are you like the person whose opinion you value?*
— *Why is it important to choose people to look up to and respect?*

Your Questions:

An Important Person in My Life

Purpose:

This topic reinforces the importance of consciously choosing people one respects as role models.

Character Traits:

Respect, Caring, Ethical Decision Making, Sociability, Positive Attitude

Introducing the Topic:

In your own words, say to the students: *The topic today is, "An Important Person in My Life." Most of us interact with many people every day. Some are friends, some are relatives, and some are strangers. The people who are important to us have usually contributed something special to our lives. For example, they may look after us, guide us, or teach us. Frequently they share our joys and sorrows.*

Tell us about one important person in your life. This person could be a parent, grandparent, teacher, counselor, or coach. He or she could also be a friend. Tell us how and why this person is important to you, and how you feel when you are with him or her. Our topic is, "An Important Person in My Life."

Discussion Questions:

— *What characteristics did our important people have in common?*
— *If your important person were no longer available to you, how would you manage to get along?*
— *What is the most important thing you have learned from this person?*

Your Questions:

I Succeeded Because I Encouraged Myself

Purpose:

This topic helps students understand the value of positive self-talk and that doubts are natural but can be overcome if we counteract them with encouraging words.

Character Traits:

Positive Attitude, Perserverance, Determination, Self-Management

Introducing the Topic:

In your own words, say to the students: *Our topic for this session is, "I Succeeded Because I Encouraged Myself." Have you ever wanted to do something and weren't quite sure you could? Think of a time when you felt unsure, but encouraged yourself and, consequently, found a way to be successful. Perhaps you tried to teach your pet a trick, or needed to do a good job on a report for school. Maybe you were trying to master something on a computer, or were learning a new game. Whatever it was, you were not sure you could do it, but after giving yourself some encouraging words, you were successful. Take a few quiet moments to think it over. The topic is, "I Succeeded Because I Encouraged Myself."*

Discussion Questions:

— What do you think caused each of you to be successful?
— What kinds of doubts did you have to overcome to be successful?
— What do you think would have happened if you had used discouraging words instead of encouraging words?
— In what other areas of you life do you think encouraging words (to yourself or others) would be helpful?

Your Questions:

Someone Tried to Make Me Do Something I Didn't Want to Do

Purpose:

This topic gives students the opportunity to examine and discuss their feelings about peer pressure, and to understand what is involved in making positive, healthy decisions.

Character Traits:

Self-Control, Self-Discipline, Responsibility, Trustworthiness, Courage, Ethical Decision Making, Integrity

Introducing the Topic:

In your own words, say to the students: *Today we are going to talk about something that has happened to many of us. Our today is, "Someone Tried to Make Me Do Something I Didn't Want to Do." Maybe you can think of a time when someone you knew—perhaps a friend or a group of friends—wanted you to go someplace or do something against your better judgment. Maybe you thought it might be harmful to you or someone else, or maybe it was illegal.*

The thing to focus on here is how you handled the situation. Did you go along with the person? If you did, how did you feel about it later? If you decided not to go along, how did you feel about that? Did it have any effect on your relationship with the person? This sort of situation can be very tough to handle; when it happens, we feel put on the spot. If you decide to share your experience, tell us what happened and how you felt, but don't tell us who was pressuring you. The topic today is, "Someone Tried to Make Me Do Something I Didn't Want to Do."

Discussion Questions:

— *What makes situations like this seem like no-win situations?*
— *Which matters more—doing what you believe is right or shielding other people from disappointment?*
— *If someone has a strong sense of personal values, do you think it's easier for him or her to say no? Why or why not?*
— *What are some ways we can learn to say no, when saying no is in our best interest?*

Your Questions:

A Significant Event in My Life

Purpose:

By focusing on an important life event, this topic enables the students to understand the connection between that event and their personal value system.

Character Traits:

Positive Attitude, Responsibility (Any values and character traits mentioned during discussion)

Introducing the Topic:

In your own words, say to the students: *Today's topic is, "A Significant Event in My Life." There are many kinds of events that hold places of significance in our memories. What is one of the most significant that you can recall? It could be an achievement, such as winning an academic or athletic event or mastering a skill, or it could be a personal triumph, such as gaining control of a habit. Your significant event might be a move you made to new city or school. Or it might be a negative event, such as the death of a pet, or a divorce in the family. Think of one event in your life that you would like to share. Our topic is, "A Significant Event in My Life."*

Discussion Questions:

— *How do negative events become significant in our lives?*
— *How do positive events become significant in our lives?*
— *Who decides how much significance an event has?*
— *How do significant events help us to identify our values?*
— *How do you think you will feel in five or ten years about events that are significant to you now?*

Your Questions:

Something I Want to Keep

Purpose:

This topic asks the students to focus on a personal item or quality in themselves that they treasure. In the process, the students identify values that are important to them.

Character Traits:

Positive Attitude, Open-Mindedness, Confidence, Excellence, Enthusiasm

Introducing the Topic:

In your own words, say to the students: *Today we are going to talk about, "Something I Want to Keep." The term keepsake is usually applied to a material object of value to us, such as a souvenir or memento from a special event, a picture of a friend or loved one, or a gift received on a special occasion. Other things we like to keep are medals, plaques, and certificates of award. You might choose to keep the ball you used to make the winning point in an important game. Or your first doll, painting, or poem. You might also want to keep an intangible thing, such as your love of animals, or your respect for the environment. Choose one tangible or intangible thing that you want to keep and tell us why it is important to you. Our topic is, "Something I Want to Keep."*

Discussion Questions:

— What similarities did you notice in the things we want to keep?
— What determines whether or not you decide to keep something?
— How will you benefit by having your keepsake to look at ten or twenty-five years from now?
— Upon what value did you base your decision to keep the thing you described?
— How do our values help us determine what's important and, therefore, what we want to keep?

Your Questions:

My Greatest Asset

Purpose:

This topic provides students an opportunity to describe, and be acknowledged for, a positive asset.

Character Traits:

Self-Discipline, Self-Management, Positive Attitude, Ethical Decision Making, Responsibility

Introducing the Topic:

In your own words, say to the students: *Today's topic is, "My Greatest Asset." Everyone has assets. In the financial world, our assets are property, stocks, cash—things that add to our wealth. Assets in our personal lives represent a different kind of wealth. They are the attributes we possess and the skills we've developed.*

What is your greatest asset? Maybe it's your intelligence or your sense of humor. It might be your loyalty or your ability to make others feel comfortable, even in new situations. Maybe you are excellent at drawing, dancing, writing, computing, or growing things. Or perhaps you are good at listening, often hearing what others are feeling but not saying. Review some of the many assets you have, and choose the one you think is your greatest. Our topic is, "My Greatest Asset."

Discussion Questions:

— *Why is it important to recognize our assets?*
— *Which are more important, personal assets or financial assets? Why?*
— *Why is it sometimes difficult to talk about ourselves positively?*

Your Questions:

Part of Me Wanted to Do One Thing, and Part of Me Wanted to Do Another

Purpose:

This topic asks students to examine conflicting desires, the values that underlie those desires, and the decision-making process used to resolve the conflict.

Character Traits:

Self-Control, Self-Discipline, Trustworthiness, Ethical Decision Making, Responsibility

Introducing the Topic:

In your own words, say to the students: *Our topic today is, "Part of Me Wanted to Do One Thing, and Part of Me Wanted to Do Another." Being torn between two choices is a common experience. Here's a typical example: One part of you—we'll call it the student part—wants to study and learn a subject well. Another part—the social part—wants to go to a party. Both parts are very real, but at times they are at odds with each other. Have you had a similar experience? Maybe you had a choice between going to a movie and going to a ball game, and part of you wanted the movie and part of you wanted the game. Or maybe you were torn between two equally tantalizing items on a lunch menu. Today let's talk about times when you were divided by a similar conflict. Take a minute and think about it. The topic is, "Part of Me Wanted to Do One Thing, and Part of Me Wanted to Do Another."*

Discussion Questions:

— What are the advantages of being a complex person with many different "parts?" What are some disadvantages?
— How did your values influence the decision you finally made?
— How can we resolve inner conflicts like these when they occur?

Your Questions:

I Said Yes When I Wanted to Say No

Purpose:

This topic encourages students to describe a time when their chosen behavior went against their true desires, and to identify the values that led to that decision.

Character Traits:

Self-Control, Self-Discipline, Responsibility, Ethical Decision Making

Introducing the Topic:

In your own words, say to the students: *Today our session is about being assertive. We're going to talk about times when we found it tough to assert ourselves. The topic is, "I Said Yes When I Wanted to Say No."*

Have you ever agreed to do something that you really didn't want to do? Maybe you agreed to attend a meeting that you really weren't interested in, or go to the park when you wanted to stay home. Or maybe someone asked to copy your homework and, instead of being assertive and saying no, you said okay. Take a moment to think about a time when something like this happened to you. The topic is, "I Said Yes When I Wanted to Say No."

Discussion Questions:

— Why do you think people say yes when they really want to say no?
— If you resent doing something you don't really want to do, but you agreed to do it, who's to blame?
— How did you feel when you did something you really didn't want to do?
— If you had said no, how would you have felt about yourself?

Your Questions:

A Way in Which I'm Responsible

Purpose:
This topic asks students to describe responsible behaviors in which they regularly engage. In the process, they develop an awareness of the value of taking responsibility and following through on commitments.

Character Traits:
Self-Management, Responsibility, Perserverence, Trustworthiness, Ethical Decision making

Introducing the Topic:
In your own words, say to the students: *The topic for today's discussion is, "A Way in Which I'm Responsible." Think of a responsibility that you accept and carry out. It may be a chore that you do each week, like sweeping the kitchen floor or watering the lawn. Perhaps your responsibility is to do your homework every evening after dinner, or to read a half hour each night before bed. Maybe you get up on time every morning, or fix breakfast for yourself and your younger brothers or sisters. Do you earn and save money? These are all ways of being responsible. Before we begin, think quietly for a few moments about something you do that is responsible. The topic is, "A Way in Which I'm Responsible."*

Discussion Questions:
— *What did you learn by hearing about the responsible things that other students do?*
— *Why do you think it is important to have responsibilities?*
— *How does being a responsible person make you feel about yourself?*

Your Questions:

A Time I Disappointed Someone

Purpose:

This topic helps students to examine, and understand the consequences of, their actions. It also helps develop an understanding of the concerns and feelings of others, and the ability to take another person's perspective.

Character Traits:

Honesty, Responsibility, Respect, Trustworthiness, Ethical Decision Making

Introducing the Topic:

In your own words, say to the students: *Our topic today is, "A Time I Disappointed Someone." Different people expect different things from us. Sometimes we know we are going to disappoint someone and it cannot be avoided. Sometimes we don't want to, hope we won't, and do anyway. There are lots of ways to disappoint someone. Think of an example from your life. Your parent might have expected you to complete a task and you didn't. A friend might have expected you to go to the movies and you couldn't. Sometimes you might even disappoint yourself! You might have expected to get an A on a book report you wrote, and then discovered that you got only a C. Maybe you told a lie and got caught. Close your eyes and think for a moment of a time when you heard those words, "I'm disappointed in you." When you are ready, our topic for discussion is, "A Time I Disappointed Someone."*

Discussion Questions:

— *How do you feel when you disappoint someone?*
— *What is the relationship between expectation and disappointment?*
— *What can you do about someone's disappointment in you?*

Your Questions:

A Time I Used Good Judgement

Purpose:
This topic challenges the students to apply a working definition of judgment in evaluating decisions they have made, as well as the consequences of those decisions.

Character Traits:
Self-Management, Determination, Responsibility, Trustworthiness, Ethical Decision Making

Introducing the Topic:
In your own words, say to the students: *The topic for this session is, "A Time I Used Good Judgement." The point of this session is to discuss times when our judgement caused us to make choices that worked out well for us. You've used good judgement lots of times. Try to remember an example that you'd feel okay about sharing. Maybe you used good judgment in the way you spent or saved some money. Perhaps you handled a touchy problem extremely well, or asked for help when you needed it. You might have found yourself in a potentially dangerous situation and made choices that preserved your health and/or safety. If you'd like to tell us about a time when you think your judgment was particularly good, we'd like to hear about it. The topic is, "A Time I Used Good Judgement."*

Discussion Questions:
— *What similarities did you notice in the things we discussed during this session?*
— *What are we really talking about when we use the term* judgment*?*
— *How do you usually feel when you know that your judgment is sound?*
— *What kinds of pressures or circumstances sometimes cause us to use bad judgment? How can we prevent such things from happening?*

Your Questions:

It Was Difficult, But I Controlled Myself

Purpose:

This topic allows students to explore times when their ability to use rational self-control overruled the need to react impulsively, reinforcing the ability of students to make sound decisions.

Character Traits:

Self-Management, Pereseverance, Determination, Responsibility, Self-Discipline, Self-Control

Introducing the Topic:

In your own words, say to the students: *The topic for today's session is "It Was Difficult, But I Controlled Myself." See if you can remember a time when you controlled your actions despite strong feelings that could have led you in a less positive direction. You may have been about to react angrily to a situation without giving your behavior much thought, but were able to gain control of yourself. It might have been a time when someone said or did something that was very upsetting, but you didn't let it get to you. Maybe you felt you were being treated unfairly or perhaps it was something like being left out of an activity or game. Think it over for a minute and remember not to share any names, just the incident. The topic for this session is "It Was Difficult, But I Controlled Myself."*

Discussion Questions:

— *How did you feel about yourself when you were able to use self-control?*
— *Sometimes we make things worse when we say or do something that makes us feel better at the moment. How can we judge when it's best to say or do what we feel like doing, and when its best to use self-control and hold ourselves back?*
— *What are some of the things we can do to maintain self-control in an emotional situation?*

Your Questions:

Someone in Authority Whom I Respect

Purpose:

In this discussion, students describe methods or styles of authority to which they respond positively. In the process, they recognize that authority figures earn respect or disrespect based on their actions.

Character Traits:

Respect, Excellence

Introducing the Topic:

In your own words, say to the students: *Our topic today is "Someone in Authority Whom I Respect." Does anyone come to mind who is in some kind of authority or leadership position and for whom you have a lot of respect? It may be someone who you know personally who is in some kind of a responsible position. It could be a teacher, parent, or a student who handles his or her leadership position well. Perhaps the person who comes to your mind is someone who holds public office, is a world leader of some kind, or a star athlete. Can any of you think of someone like this? Tell us who the person is that you respect; why it is that you respect him or her; and try to identify the specific things he or she says and does that you respect. Take a minute to think about it. The topic is "Someone in Authority Whom I Respect."*

Discussion Questions:

— Does "respect" mean the same as "like" to you? Explain.
— If you were in an authority position, how would you gain respect?
— Why is it important for someone in authority to earn the respect of others?
— What are some things that can lead to a loss of respect?

Your Questions:

I Could Have Hurt Someone's Feelings, But I Didn't

Purpose:

This topic asks students to describe a time when they made a conscious decision to spare the feelings of another, and to identify the reasons behind their decision.

Character Traits:

Empathy, Respect, Caring, Self-Control, Ethical Decision Making, Compassion

Introducing the Topic:

In your own words, say to the students: *Today our topic is, "I Could Have Hurt Someone's Feelings, But I Didn't." We have all been in situations where we could have said or done something to hurt another person. This sort of situation presents itself frequently, for a variety of reasons. Think about a time when you were in this position. Maybe someone said or did something that wasn't appropriate, and you could easily have corrected or criticized the person, but for some reason you decided against it. Perhaps you heard someone exaggerate or lie in order to impress people, but you decided not to let on that you knew the truth. Or when someone made an embarrassing mistake, perhaps you bit your tongue and didn't laugh. Your decision might have been based on friendship, or fear that the person might hurt you back, or your realization that what the person was going through at that moment wasn't easy. Think about an experience you've had like this and, without telling us who the person was, share what happened. Our topic is, "I Could Have Hurt Someone's Feelings, But I Didn't."*

Discussion Questions:

— *What were some of the things that kept us from hurting other people's feelings?*
— *How did you feel about yourself for making the choice not to hurt someone's feelings?*
— *What was the most important thing you learned in this session?*

Your Questions:

A Time I Accepted and Included Someone

Purpose:
This topic helps students to understand the need of all people to belong and feel accepted by others while identifying specific behaviors that demonstrate acceptance.

Character Traits:
Open-Mindedness, Generosity. Tolerance, Empathy, Respect, Caring, Courage, Ethical Decision Making, Sociability, Compassion

Introducing the Topic:
In your own words, say to the students: *People want to be treated in friendly ways by others. Everyone needs to feel liked, and most everyone wants to be invited to play or participate with others. Yet sometimes it's hard for us to accept a new person. So today, let's talk about times we were friendly to someone who needed our friendship—even if it felt uncomfortable. Our topic is, "A Time I Accepted and Included Someone." Can you remember a time like that? It could have happened here at school, in your neighborhood, or at church. Perhaps someone new came along and you were nice to that person because you knew how he or she felt. Maybe you were the new person yourself once, and you remembered how much you wanted to be accepted and included. Or maybe the person you accepted and included was someone you'd had a disagreement with, and you wanted the person to know you still liked him or her. If you decide to share, tell us how you demonstrated your acceptance. Think about it for a few moments. When you are ready, look up at me and we'll start the session. The topic is, "A Time I Accepted and Included Someone."*

Discussion Questions:
— How did you feel about yourself when you accepted and Included this person?
— What does it mean to people when we accept and include them?
— Why is it hard sometimes to show someone acceptance and to include him or her?

Your Questions:

A Promise That Was Hard to Keep

Purpose:

This topic helps students to recognize that promises should not be made lightly, and that the respect of others, as well as themselves, often rests on their ability to keep their commitments and promises.

Character Traits:

Self-Managment, Self-Control, Determination, Responsibility, Trustworthiness, Ethical Decision Making, Integrity, Honesty

Introducing the Topic:

In your own words, say to the students: *Today, our topic is, "A Promise That Was Hard To Keep." Notice that this is a topic that allows you to go either way. You can talk about how you kept your promise, or you can talk about a promise that proved too difficult to keep. When we make a promise, we are pledging our word. But sometimes we agree to something that, although it may not have seemed overwhelming at first, proves very difficult in the long run. Other times, we know right from the start that it will be tough, but for some reason we promise anyway. Think of a promise that you found hard to keep and tell us the circumstances, the outcome, and your feelings along the way. Please remember not to use names. The topic is, "A Promise That Was Hard to Keep."*

Discussion Questions:

— *How do you feel about yourself when you are able to keep a promise? ... not able to keep a promise?*
— *How does the other person feel about you when you keep a promise? ... when you fail to keep a promise?*
— *How are promises related to honesty, integrity, and trust?*
— *What should you do if someone asks for a promise that you can't honestly make?*

Your Questions:

I Said No Because It Was the Right Thing to Do

Purpose:

This topic invites students to identify a time when they made a decision based on a moral value rather than on personal gratification or convenience.

Character Traits:

Self-Discipline, Self-Management, Determination, Responsibility, Trustworthiness, Courage, Ethical Decision Making, Integrity

Introducing the Topic:

In your own words, say to the students: *Has anyone ever asked you to do something that you knew was wrong or not good for you? Maybe the thing this person asked you to do sounded like fun, so it was hard to say no—but you did. Things like that happen to all of us, not just while we are growing up, but even as adults, so it's important to learn to say no. Today, let's talk about how we can do that. Our topic is, "I Said No Because It Was The Right Thing To Do." Think of a time when you really wanted to do something, but you knew you shouldn't, so you said no. Maybe a friend asked you to come over after school, but your mother wanted you to come straight home, so you said no. Or maybe someone asked you to trade your sandwich for a candy bar, but you knew that wouldn't be a good lunch, so you said no. Did anyone ever ask you to tell a lie so he or she wouldn't get into trouble? Or keep quiet about something? Or smoke a cigarette? Tell us about something like this that happened to you, but don't say who asked you to do it. Think about it for a moment or two, and look at me when you are ready to share. The topic is, "I Said No Because It Was The Right Thing To Do."*

Discussion Questions:

— How did you feel about yourself when you said no?
— What did the other person do or say when you said no?
— Why is it hard to say no?
— How can we learn to say no to people who ask us to do things that are wrong or bad for us?
— Once you've said no to something you know you shouldn't do, is it a little easier the next time you are confronted with a similar situation? Why or why not?

How My Mistake Helped Me Learn

Purpose:

This topic encourages students to recognize that everyone make mistakes from time to time and to understand that mistakes don't mean failure. It also helps students to view mistakes as learning experiences.

Character Traits:

Self-Management, Open-Mindedness, Perseverance, Responsibility, Self-Discipline, Positive Attitude, Ethical Decision Making

Introducing the Topic:

In your own words, say to the students: *When we make choices, we sometimes choose the wrong thing. We call this making a mistake. Our topic today is, "How My Mistake Helped Me Learn." We all make mistakes—and we all have a chance to learn something from every mistake we make. Mistakes are like good friends—they teach us things we need to know. Think of a mistake you made that taught you something. It could have been a big mistake, or a small one. For example, maybe you tried to spell a new word and used the wrong letter, but making that mistake helped you learn to spell the word correctly. Or maybe you asked for a great big piece of cake with ice cream, and when your stomach hurt afterwards, you learned not to take so much next time. Maybe when you were very young you wandered off in the shopping center and lost your parents for a while. How did you find them again, and what did you learn? Maybe you left your bike outside overnight and in the morning it was gone. What did that mistake teach you? Think quietly for a few minutes. Think of a mistake you made, and then think about what you learned from making it. Look at me when you're ready to share. The topic is, "How My Mistake Helped Me Learn."*

Discussion Questions:

— *Why do mistakes happen?*
— *Why is it OK to make mistakes?*
— *What can mistakes teach us about ourselves?*
— *If we let them, can mistakes be our friends? How?*

Your Questions:

If your heart is in Social-Emotional
Learning, visit us online.

Come see us at
www.InnerchoicePublishing.com

Our web site gives you a look at all our other Social-Emotional Learning-based books, free activities, articles, research, and learning and teaching strategies. Every week you'll get a new Sharing Circle topic and lesson.

INNERCHOICE Publishing
15079 Oak Chase Court
Wellington, FL 33414

www.ingramcontent.com/pod-product-compliance
Lightning Source LLC
Chambersburg PA
CBHW080517110426
42742CB00017B/3147